Racism and Human Rights

Edited by Raphael Walden

The Consultative Council of
Jewish Organizations
And the Shoresh Charitable Trust

Springer Science+Business Media, B.V.
2004

A C.I.P. Catalogue record for this book is available from the Library of Congress.

Printed on acid-free paper.

ISBN 978-90-04-13651-9 ISBN 978-94-017-6031-7 (eBook)
DOI 10.1007/978-94-017-6031-7

Typeset by jules guldenmund layout & text, The Hague

Table of Contents

Preface 1
Clemens Nathan

Racism, Xenophobia and Discrimination—
Humanity's Need for a New Ethical Code of Conduct 7
His Royal Highness Prince El Hassan Bin Talal

The Security Council and the Protection of Human Rights 15
Bertrand G. Ramcharan

The Future Shape of Europe 31
Robert Badinter

Slavery as Piracy—The Legal Case for Reparations for Slavery 41
Geraldine Van Bueren

Judaism as a Source of Human Rights 55
Asher Maoz

Perceptions of the Other—Lessons from Jewish-Christian Dialogue 85
Edward Kessler

Racism and Xenophobia in Virtual Russia 101
Stella Rock

Unease in the Global Village: German-language Racism on the Internet 125
Rebekah Webb

The European Race Directive: A Bridge so Far? 143
Fernne Brennan

The Drafting of the Articles on the Middle East and Antisemitism at the Durban Conference Against Racism 165
Raphael Walden

Preface

Clemens Nathan*

Conflict prevention is a duty of every non-governmental organization working to improve understanding between peoples and countries. It is often an overlooked element of the work of non-governmental organizations dedicated to protecting human rights around the world. The work of these organisations has helped to form the concepts and standards which have been embodied in treaties and common institutions. Human rights workers must pay constant attention to the inevitably conflicting interests and divergent understandings of those most interested in the process of promoting and protecting human values. Nowhere is this more evident than in the United Nations. Political tensions and conflicts clash with the high-minded idealism of those wishing to ensure liberty, dignity and equality for all. These questions are as pertinent today as they were in the classical texts or the political philosophy of the past. None have succeeded in providing a practical model in which the dignity, rights and duties of the individual can be removed from the realm of political conflict. In our day, the widespread desire to see progress towards the better protection of our human rights compels us to reflect upon the significance of the conflict and compromise so evident in the international institutions created to watch over the fulfilment of our ideals.

---

* Chairman of the CCJO and former President of the Anglo-Jewish Association. Honorary fellow of the Centre for Jewish-Christian Relations at Cambridge University, England.

Raphael Walden (ed.), Racism and Human Rights, *1-6.*

It is evident that much of the controversy over international human rights norms is linked to deeper tensions between cherished ideals. Under the treaties and agreements of the United Nations, no man or woman should be molested on account of his or her opinions, provided that avowal of them does not disturb the public order established by law, and provided that liberty is not abused. But how do we define the 'public order', 'law' and 'liberty' rightfully enjoyed by an individual? Tensions between the rights of individuals and the community have exercised some of our greatest philosophers. There is still no practical consensus for modern statesmen to act upon. Earlier modern thinkers such as John Locke, sought to solve this problem through positing the existence of a 'social contract' underpinning the law, a contract between individuals and the representatives of different social interests, who voluntarily placed themselves under a sovereign's rule. They should nevertheless have retained those customary or 'ancient' liberties which did not touch upon the needs for public order by a sovereign. The 'social contract' theory gained widespread adherence, but it provided little intellectual ground for a consensus on which rights might be suspended and when. As modern states and the world economy developed further, the need to understand an ever-wider range of political, economic and social factors concentrated the thoughts of political philosophers on the role to be played by the rights and freedoms of individuals and communities in the continued functioning of the state itself. During the nineteenth century, liberal thinkers began to assert that freedom was such an essential element of active and responsible citizenship that a state could only prosper by carefully nourishing the rights of the individual. The nineteenth-century liberals who agreed that the state's authority was tied to its ability to give individuals opportunities to exercise their rights and duties did not move towards any great consensus on the natural limits of the rights of the individual, nor did they provide a basis for minorities within society to enjoy any distinctive civil or political rights deriving from their distinctive cultures or lifestyles. Individualist thinkers such as John Stuart Mill appeared unduly over-optimistic about the historic trend towards the fulfilment of the individual. The rise of socialist and communist movements in the nineteenth and twentieth centuries, the tragedies of the First and Second World Wars, and conflicts based on nationalism highlighted the failures of these philosophical ideals.

René Cassin, one of the main draftsmen of the Universal Declaration of Human Rights in 1948, was one of the clearest thinkers in this field. He experienced the two world wars, and their inhumanity and horrific ideological conflicts, and argued that disparate ideologies would not of themselves fit into the lasting solutions which political philosophers had always highlighted. He sought to balance the need for public order and respect for the liberty of the individual. Cassin became Chairman of the UN Commission on Human Rights, where he argued that human rights could only be realised when looked at as a product of a combination of the influences on human lives. He emphasized that people are members of communities and social groups as well as being individuals with distinctive interests that cannot be reduced to communal or national identifications. No ideology will be able to encompass the diversity of interests in which humans are naturally engaged, and therefore Cassin sought to sidestep the ideologies of the past and present by holding that individual and collective aspirations are equally valid, focusing on practical means to address conflicts between rights to security and to freedom.

The Human Rights concepts of the United Nations which Cassin helped to create, embody the inevitable tension between our common ideals and the practical realities of power and politics created by the search for peace and freedom, security and rights. Those working with the United Nations will inevitably be frustrated by the political conflicts associated with its highly complex structure. Nevertheless, experience shows how non-governmental organizations such as ours can, with other representatives of international public opinion, help the UN institutions to highlight and address infringements affecting individual and collective human rights. Building upon the Universal Declaration of Human Rights, the UN has made extremely important advances in the protection of human rights through international treaties, focusing international attention on unacceptable conditions faced by people in all parts of the world. Many well-intended developments are misused for political ends; one must constantly be on guard. A compromise can be so far-reaching that new agreements may have no value at all. In Cassin's time at the Commission on Human Rights, his approach to sidestepping or outflanking Cold War ideologues created some of the most important improvements in the UN's human rights treaty system. Since the Universal Declaration, the UN has set down a host of treaties and agreements which may serve as boundaries beyond which the representatives of dissenting states may not attempt to lead the international community. Today, as in the twentieth century, many ideologues are still willing to countenance the murder of millions, in order to advance the 'rights' of others. In our day, after the failure of a succession of horrific ideologies, the defenders of human rights must remember that no ideology guarantees enough security or fulfillment ever to justify such distortions of human rights. There is no one ideology for us all. The adherents of failed ideologies were defeated because they could not produce stable, fair and decent societies for all, nor would they allow people to determine how their own countries should be run. Faced with the kind of false logic employed by such authoritarians, the United Nations must today make grave choices, in order to retain a concept of human rights and dignity with which the majority of nations will be able to identify in the twenty-first century.

The essays in this book highlight many of the problems for those who seek to balance individual and collective rights and security as they affect us today. His Royal Highness Prince El Hassan bin Talal underlines the need for an intercultural dialogue to strengthen the global ethic which underpins our concept of human rights. Where so many have baulked at the task of relating human rights to specific religious or cultural ethics, Prince Hassan affirms that this may be done without jeopardy to the universal application of a rights-based ethic, and without losing sight of the rights of the individual in society. Dr. Bertrand Ramcharan shows how the Security Council has come to be increasingly involved in the implementation of human rights standards, a role originally envisaged for it in the work of the late René Cassin. Robert Badinter's paper highlights the original contribution to international constitutional law which the new Constitution of Europe wil bring to the European Parliament. It will be unlike any other constitution and will try to achieve a balance between protecting the sovereignty of individual member states while at the same time preserving and strenghtening the European Union's authority. Professor Geraldine van Buren looks at the historical development of international law, to offer a classic model for dealing with reparations for victims of slavery, developed long before modern human rights theorists turned to the problem. Professor Asher Maoz explores some of the tensions created when traditional Jewish ethics come into contact with the modern state, noting that modern human rights theory has derived much from traditional religious philosophy, and that this legacy may still work to strengthen public appreciation of the nature of and need to encourage respect for human rights, without undermining theological beliefs. Using the very specific dialogue between Christians and Jews as a reference point, Dr Edward Kessler shows how the modern concept of a respectful dialogue can transform historic enmity into a fruitful and dynamic relationship, allowing individuals from both parties to define themselves in radically different ways, and without conflict. Dr Stella Rock and Rebekah Webb, focusing on racism on the internet, show how speedily this modern technology has been adopted by some of the most insular and dangerous elements of our global society, subverting a tool available to all, and whose contribution to the information age might otherwise be expected to strengthen our democracies. Their work shows how a transnational network of racists is developing links and re-formulating ideologies, asserting rights through brutal attempts to abuse the rights and security of others. Internet racism is clearly a changing phenomenon, and the attempt of the UN to address it will be one of the most difficult tasks for proponents of human rights with an eye to the wider international implications of the medium and its message. Freedom of speech here needs to be clearly defined and not perverted. Dr Ferne Brennan investigates the strengths and weaknesses of the 'European Race Directive', an instrument designed to cover the whole of the European Union and which will have to be adapted to the very different cultures, societies and legal traditions of member states. After the Nice conference, this will be especially important. Finally, Raphael Walden has described the way in which the Durban Conference on Racism was to a considerable degree sidetracked from its true purpose by the introduction of inappropriate discussions about the Middle East, while downplaying the far more relevant issue of antisemitism.

Earlier versions of the papers appearing in this book were circulated among many international organisations at the UN Conference on Racism in Durban in 2001. Demand for them has been remarkable, and it was felt that it would be a useful contribution to the understanding of the problems highlighted in the papers to publish them in book form.

It is our fervent hope that, despite the dreadful abuses of the UN's antiracist and wider human rights objectives which occurred in Durban, decency and truth will prevail, allowing the international human rights community to strengthen its real work against racism, in all its forms. As the UN turns its attention to more and more abuses of the rights of ethnic groups and minorities, those who benefit from the repression and scapegoating of others will inevitably attempt to block the UN's anti-racist programmes. Many new immigrants, ethnic groups and minorities have made extraordinary contributions to their societies which enrich everyone. Their rights must surely be of benefit to others. Those who see themselves as human rights activists must be made to see the absurdity of scapegoating others and fomenting racist hatred as part of their strategies. Durban underlined the extent to which political objectives can make the demonisation of Jews a contemporary rather an historical injustice. The C.C.J.O. is at one with those more enlightened human rights advocates who seek to resolve political differences over the implementation of our common ideals through dialogue and compromise, whose commitment to the international institutions created for conflict resolution and the maintenance of human rights and international law opposes the kind of ideological fanaticism seen in Durban, and who believe that human beings with diverse traditions can live side by side and enrich one another's lives and understanding. Today, in the communication age, the international community has a multitude of instruments aimed at increasing respect for the different ways in which people can strive for liberty and security, despite their diverse ideologies and beliefs. If we do not take up the challenge of using the new forms of international communication for the real benefit of mankind, we shall instead be handing these new technological tools over to fanatics committed to hatred and conflict, who claim to speak in the name of the very values of dignity, rights and peace upon which they trample.

Racism, Xenophobia and Discrimination—Humanity's Need for a New Ethical Code of Conduct

His Royal Highness Prince El Hassan Bin Talal of the Hashemite Kingdom of Jordan

Introduction

The Holy Qur'an says, 'We have made you nations and tribes that you may know one another .. not that you may despise one another'. The Holy Prophet Muhammad (peace be with him and his progeny) set out the egalitarian precepts of Islam as law with moral and ethical dimensions in addition to legal ones. Thus, from the very outset—and indeed inherent to its message—Islam rejected any notion of differences based upon racial or ethnic distinction, and thus also rejected any notions of discrimination that might be based upon such differences. The Holy Prophet was forthright in explicating the message that mankind would be judged according to their humanity, and emphasized that 'No Arab is above a non-Arab' just as 'No white is above black', and vice versa. In sum, racism, which is very clearly defined in the Oxford American Dictionary as, 'Belief in the superiority of a particular race; prejudice based

Raphael Walden (ed.), Racism and Human Rights, *7-14.*

on this racism and antagonism towards other races', is a scourge and an evil. The message, as born out by meetings prior to the World Conference Against Racism, has to be to focussed on fostering a culture of pluralism and respect for diversity. Although Islam does not believe in the notion of race Muslims are forced to confront racism as a reality they are experiencing. Antimuslimism may be twinned at times to antisemitism, but Muslims are facing a double discrimination, both racial and religious.

But racism has to be dealt with globally as well as locally and transnationally. Throughout history, people have split the world into two camps: us and them. Phobias—Islamophobia, antimuslimism, semitophobia, antisemitism, xenophobia, racism, racial discrimination and apartheid—are all, by their very definition, irrational terms. The world today is interconnected and intradependant. A culture of peace is long overdue. Although agreements and treaties have long been recognized as essential instruments for regulating the conduct of states, far less attention has been given to a more comprehensive approach engaging individuals—the citizens of those same states. In Tehran, Iran, in February, 2001, during the Preparatory Conference for Durban, despite expounding the idea of a Code of Conduct, despite promoting the importance of involving civil society, and despite maintaining that it was vital in such processes to involve the Non-Governmental Organizations (NGOs), the latter were, in the end, given only a meagre and disappointing ten minutes to speak. It is therefore tragic that the involvement of the common man is not encouraged. Addressing the cause of despair—the economic, social and political causes of despair—by inviting people to participate in such fora is an important point of departure if one is to underline the importance of the right to a dignified life free from terror and free from despair.

Islamophobia

Islamophobia has recent and not so recent roots. In 1995, *The New York Times* speculated in its first day of reporting on why terrorists would have struck in Oklahoma City: 'Some Middle Eastern groups have held meetings there, and the city is home to at least three mosques.' In the 1800s, Ernest Renan's thesis was also that the world of the Muslim was a closed one, incapable of absorbing rationalist thought.

The Runnymede Commission in the UK a few years ago described Islamophobia as 'marked by a brazen hostility, bordering on contempt, for the most cherished principles of Islamic life and thought, reaching an apoplexy of hate in the modern Western media who represent Islam as intolerant of diversity, monolithic and war-mongering'. It went on: 'Islamophobia is a challenge not only to Muslims in the West but to all thinking people who are trying to grapple with complex problems of civilizational friction and conflict'.

Saeid Reza Ameli, of the Islamic Centre of England, extended the idea of Islamophobia and spoke, in 1997, of Eurocentrism, which he described as anti-universalist since although it paradoxically claims the universalist high moral ground that imitation of the Western model by all the peoples of the world is the only solution to the challenges of our time. Eurocentrism, a specifically modern phenomenon, is founded upon a racialistic viewpoint, which is rooted in the phobia of Islam.

Code of Conduct and New Global Ethic

There has to be a new concept—a code of conduct—that should not only be based on rationality and scientific method but should also consider the importance of values. It takes years of conversation to develop rules of conduct and to appreciate the religious dimensions of interfaith dialogue. At Durban, and at future follow-ups to this unique event, Muslim people of faith need to contribute, along with other people of faith but Christian and Jewish people of faith in particular, interpretations of, and contributions to, Racism and Discrimination. We should emphasize beginning with commonality, because those worlds are the worlds in which we share. And beginning with commonality includes addressing the international agenda of today. The agenda of the participation of civil society needs democratic social interaction. It exists outside the boundaries of the family but lies short of the state. It involves organizing virtually everything that happens between individual citizens and the state that is non-violent. In reference to such a code, we should embrace the Principle of Non-Coercion (Islam is very clear on there being no compulsion in religion, for example). Thus, if in a matter of belief there shall be no compulsion in religion, we should naturally attempt to focus on working for something rather than against something. Conversation is not between faiths, it is between the adherents of the faiths. I respect what is sacred to you and I expect you to return the civility. But it is essential that we develop a value system in which we can share. Dialogue among cultures, a mutual understanding of the other, may have prevented many of the conflicts based on ethnicity and xenophobia. Building the defences of peace requires the education and the enlightenment of others.

We need a universal ethic of human understanding. This is not new, it is already in the United Nations parlance. This concept of a humanitarian ethic underlines the importance of beginning that suggested code of conduct with commonality.

The UN Secretary-General, Mr Kofi Annan, has spoken of the need for an injection of ethics, a spiritual ethos, into the UN and world bodies. To support this is to recognize the holistic nature of faith towards realizing a common humanity and moving forward towards the challenges that face us as a human family. The fight against intolerance can only be intensified if the diversity of humankind, in all its aspects, including spiritual, is appreciated. It is at the spiritual level that we often find the common ground.

In terms of a code of conduct, we should speak of the importance of upholding the right to proclaim one's own religion, for example. Enlightenment and Human Rights are inherent to assuming a code of conduct in practice. Going back to the African spiritual renaissance, one notes that despite admitting that colonialism denied human rights to human beings who were subdued by violence and kept, by force, in a state of misery and ignorance, it was necessary for the African spiritualist to 'be enriched by the infinite variety' of others.

The concept of a rainbow nation is very much a part of this spirit, and it is part of the spirit of the new South Africa, a country where, arguably, one can see just such an ethic of human understanding developing.

Gender is particularly relevant to Combating Racism and Racial Discrimination. Women all over the world remain disenfranchized, not involved, and to reconsider the content of education as part of a code of conduct is vital if women are to benefit. As long ago as 1911, the following was said at the opening of the Lucknow Muslim Girls' School: 'No community can progress if its mothers are illiterate and unable to give adequate advice, adequate guidance, to their children', a latter-day equivalent of Ruby Mannekin's oft-quoted remark, 'Educate the man you educate a person, educate a woman and you educate a family'. The Holy Prophet, the father of four daughters, believed that, 'Heaven lieth at the feet of thy mothers', and he lost no opportunity to make a favourable comment about the status of women, stating very clearly that, 'Searching for knowledge is the duty of every believer, male and female'. The Holy Qur'an also addresses both men and women equally, describing women as 'half of humanity'.

And with that injunction, searching for knowledge is indeed an imperative that is recognized by all people of faith. In this context, it is necessary to ensure a free flow of information. There is, at present, no lateral thinking on this and related issues. There is no south/south flow of information, as there should be. In speaking of a code of conduct, we are courageously looking afresh at our own and each others' texts, heritage and history. There is in this a necessary free flow of information.

In 2000, I visited Auschwitz. It was said to me at the time, 'Why are you going to do that, can't you see the horrors of what is happening in different parts of the world?' And one had to point out that one went there to make it very clear that the genocide has not ended in many different parts of the world; to make it clear that, whereas there is a Western feeling of guilt over the suffering of Jews in the Second World War, unfortunately the feeling of brotherhood, the feeling of that ethic of human solidarity, has not yet carried over to peoples of other nations. It is moving to think that 12 million people died during World War II and yet the young still speak of the 'other' in terms of colour, or in terms of race. Thus, this coming together, this looking afresh, at our own and each others' texts, heritage and history might be to triangulate the relationship, rather than leaving it in the strict bilateral context. The Catholic participant at Auschwitz said, 'We are glad that you came, because our conversation is very direct and very narrow'; and a Jewish participant said, "We hope that this will never happen again". Of course, as we look at what is happening in terms of daily violence in the Middle East, one's heart is heavy with the fact that we were not, as yet, successful in developing a people-to-people peace.

It is this ethic of human solidarity that attracted me to the work and principles of Dr Martin Luther King Jr, who said, in his *Strength to Love* (1963):

> Like an unchecked cancer, that corrodes the personality and eats away its vital unity, hate destroys a man's sense of values and his objectivity. It causes him to describe the beautiful as ugly and the ugly as beautiful, and to confuse the true with the false and the false with the true. Darkness cannot drive out darkness; only light can do that. Hate cannot drive out hate; only love can do that. Hate multiplies hate, violence multiplies violence, and toughness multiplies toughness in a descending spiral of destruction... The chain reaction of evil—hate begetting hate, wars producing more wars—must be broken, or we shall be plunged into the dark abyss of annihilation.

There are, one might suggest, three forms of fear: a fear of the other, a fear of our own kind, and a fear of making agreements public. Is it possible, or conceivable, to shake hands with an enemy? Will we be censured if we shake hands and exchange views? How do we make our feelings known to the world that we are committed to peace? It might be that we fear peace. In terms of a code of conduct, we need to develop a civilized framework for disagreement. So that when people ask, 'Why are you killing each other?', at least we can go back and say (not that one is justifying the killing of the other) that somewhere in our distant memory there was some logic to it all. What is also important in the code of conduct is to accept responsibility for words and actions at all levels.

Globalization

The term 'globalization'—that societies and individuals try to both interact with and benefit from—is understood in many parts of the world as another definition of imperialism. In many parts of the world, unless we recognize the culture of the other, human rights are also understood as carrying a particular agenda. Today, in an age of globalization, modernity, post-modernity and democracy, we are reminded of the significance of consensus. But it is well to remember that there can be no consensus without pluralism. Imam Ibrahim bin Moussa Shatibi, the erudite Muslim scholar, pointed out long ago very clearly the importance of elevating consensus and respecting differences. In the Preparatory Declaration, signed by Mrs Mary Robinson and President Nelson Mandela, which was entitled, '*Tolerance and Diversity: A Vision for the 21st Century*', the invocation was for a shared vision for an inclusive non-racial and non-discriminatory world. They invited governments and societies to take stock of how we are progressing and achieving these ideals.

Conclusion

In the late 1980s, the United Nations renewed its commitment to a new international humanitarian order. A global world needs a global ethic. It needs to address the empowerment of the poor; it needs to help develop civil society and promote politics for the people—anthropolitics; it needs to promote global governance with a human face. A Byzantine Sophist had on his epitaph, at the height of the Byzantine Empire: 'I was touched by the love of the public good, of the common good'. That common good is what we have to find once again. Can we move from a culture of involvement to a culture of service; from a culture of existing to a culture of participation? The cornerstones of such movements are respect for life, a responsibility towards future generations, the protection of the human habitat and a move away from acquisitivism towards altruism, an altruism as nurtured by a sense of mutual interest and a mutual recognition of human dignity and worth.

It is wise to again reiterate the words of the Holy Qur'an:

> *We have made you nations and tribes that you may know one another... not that you may despise one another"*

That is why we are here—to know each other, to know each other's points of departure, to agree to disagree, to be different, to be various, to accept that the concept and idea of the oneness of humanity (Tawhid) is Islam's unique contribution to human civilization: Unity of God, Unity of Creation, Unity of purpose in promoting the good and fighting the evil.

> *And among his signs is the creation of the heavens and earth and the variations and diversity of your tongues and of your colours varying in their assigns for those who know.*

Today, apart from the World Conference Against Racism, the United Nations and members of the international community are engaged in a dialogue among civilizations. According to the Princeton-based scholar and former Pakistani High Commissioner to the United Kingdom, Professor Akbar S Ahmed, Islam's roots are, in fact, in dialogue. When the Islamic tidal wave left Arabia it was immediately involved in a dialogue with civilizations. Indeed, dialogue is rooted in Islam. Yet the debate is stifled because the Muslim world is reduced to caricature. Likewise, the West in the eyes of the Muslim world is often reduced to caricature. Misconceptions are therefore mutual and excessive, not to mention mutually destructive. It is, alas, often the dialogue between the deaf, the dumb and the blind.

A code of conduct is about human dignity, and although one might argue that human dignity is an abstract, it is a reality in terms of the need to recognize the human dimension, which is an extranational dimension as opposed to a binational one. It needs to involve the forces of change: new nations, peoples' movements, women, youth. It must focus on the most vulnerable groups among us. It must listen to the witnesses of torture, of uprootedness, of neglect. It must continue to emphasize moral authority, however important political power may be.

In terms of globalization and its relevance for people of faith, and for its relevance to the World Conference Against Racism, culture should never be thought of as merely an afterthought—after security and economy. Culture is identity, culture is security, culture is the meaning of life to so many of us. Any new worldwide proposal, such as Globalization, or a new humanitarian order, or a new global ethic, or global governance, in order to have legitimacy for all concerned, must be related to the various religious, cultural and legal traditions. If this can be done, globalization will not be perceived as a western imposition on the rest of humankind. Globalization will be accepted as a way to modernize and enlarge, through participation, each tradition while remaining faithful to its roots. By the same token, each tradition will discover that the challenges human beings faced for centuries were met in more or less similar ways. In doing so, different civil societies might be inclined to accept the other as a brother sharing the same human destiny and not as a potential enemy or barbarian.

The World Conference against Racism promises to focus on action-oriented and practical steps to eradicate racism, including measures of prevention, education and protection and the provision of effective remedies. This unique 'opportunity to create a new world vision for the fight against racism in the 21st century' should not be lost on people of faith.

The Security Council and the Protection of Human Rights

Bertrand G. Ramcharan*

Introduction

The human rights idea is shaping the contemporary world. At long last, human rights are being given the prominence they deserve by the organs of the international community dealing with questions of peace and security as well as development. How is the Security Council dealing with human rights imperatives? What does it see as the place of human rights in conflict prevention, peace-making, peace-keeping and peace-building? How does the Security Council address the quest for justice in the face of gross violations of human rights?

These are some of the questions we shall explore in this presentation dedicated to René Cassin, a great architect of the International Bill of Human Rights. Let us, at the outset, look at the place René Cassin foresaw for the Security Council in the United Nations scheme for protecting human rights.

---

* Acting United Nations High Commissioner for Human Rights, a position with the rank of Under-Secretary-General. Lecture delivered to the CCJO on 2 May 2002. The views expressed are those of the author in his personal capacity.

Raphael Walden (ed.), Racism and Human Rights, *15-30.*

I. René Cassin and the Role of the Security Council in the Protection of Human Rights

In 1951, three years after the adoption of the Universal Declaration of Human Rights, René Cassin gave a course of lectures at the Hague Academy of International Law on the Universal Declaration and the Implementation of Human Rights.[1] He discussed what he considered to be innovations introduced by the Charter of the United Nations. Among these, he gave prominence to the role of the principal organs of the United Nations in the international protection of human rights. As far as the Security Council was concerned, he saw a role for the Council when the maintenance of peace could be threatened by violations of human rights. He cited in this connection articles 24, 34 and 39 of the Charter.[2] Professor Cassin considered that after the entry into force of the International Covenant on Human Rights (then being drafted) the competent organs of the United Nations and, for our purposes, the Security Council could be seized by a State of situations or complaints involving gross violations of human rights.[3]

It will thus be seen that this drafter of the Universal Declaration foresaw a role for the Security Council in the protection of human rights in situations involving a threat to international peace and security. This was consistent with his views in general on the relationship between human rights and human security—a topic that came up in his early submissions to the Commission on Human Rights at its very first session. We shall look at this next.

II. Human Rights and Human Security in the Conception of René Cassin

At the first session of the Commission on Human Rights in 1947, Professor Cassin began to lay the groundwork that would help shape the subsequent International Bill of Human Rights. As the summary records of the 7th Meeting of the Commission on Friday, 31 January 1947, recorded it,

> The representative of France stated that the concept of man as a community and man as an individual should become fused and that human rights should be respected by every State in the world. A significant example in that respect was the meeting of the ideas of France and the Union of Soviet Socialist Republics: the philosophical con-

---

1. 79 RCADI, 1951 (II), pp. 245-295.
2. *Ibid.*, p.249.
3. *Ibid.*, p.331.

> ception of the Union of Soviet Socialist Republics showed, indeed, that there was no incompatibility between the rights of man within the framework of the State and the possibility to assert himself outside the State.[4]

At the next meeting of the Commission, in the afternoon of that very day, René Cassin argued that the proposed International Bill of Human Rights ought to take account of prevailing conditions and of the political and social evolution that had transpired over the last two centuries. The records continued:

> He approved of the attempts which had been made to classify the rights according to their nature, or according to the ideas of liberty, equality and security to which they correspond. He wished to see the Commission draw up an International Bill which would be the counterpart of the present national declarations, rather than a detailed code.[5]

Professor Cassin considered it essential that the principle of equality be defined from the outset. He recalled that Hitler had started by asserting the inequality of man before attacking men's liberties:

> The principles of the unity of the human race and of the equality of men before the law should appear in one of the fundamental articles of the declaration.[6]

Professor Cassin continued to emphasize the fundamentals:

> As regards the right to existence, for example, the fundamental consideration was to assure the protection of human life… He considered that it was of fundamental importance to affirm the right of human beings to existence. Similarly, it was a fundamental duty to assert that slavery was a shame to humanity. The most elementary rights must be reaffirmed as experience has proved that they could be violated.[7]

Professor Cassin had an eye on norms as well as implementation. At the 16th meeting of the first session of the Commission on Human Rights, on 5 February 1947, he 'questioned whether the fact that there was no organ capable of replying to communications might not have an adverse effect on the prestige of the United Nations, especially in view of the great number of communications received.'[8]

---

4. E/CN.4/SR.7, p. 5.
5. E/CN.4/SR.8, p.5.
6. E/CN.4/SR.13, p.4.
7. E/CN.SR.13, p.7.
8. E/CN.SR.16, p.7.

On 6 December 1947, Professor Cassin submitted a letter to the Working Party on the Implementation of Human Rights that met during the second session of the Commission. Addressing the issue of implementation, he reminded the Commission that it was essential to bear in mind that it and the organs of the United Nations should assure respect for human rights in pursuance of the Charter. It was important, he said, that the normal courts in each country be able to provide effective remedies to those whose rights are at risk.

Professor Cassin foresaw that the International Court of Justice would be vested eventually with jurisdiction for the protection of human rights in a special Chamber. He submitted that petitions and complaints should be examined by independent persons of eminent repute appointed by the United Nations with powers of enqiry. He foresaw investigating commissions and a role for the principal organs of the United Nations, including the General Assembly, the Security Council, the Economic and Social Council, and the International Court of Justice. Professor Cassin concluded:

> Finally, I would draw the Working Parties' attention to the advisability of gradually increasing the means of implementation—by urging the importance of preventive measures which depend largely on the collaboration of States with the United Nations and the vigilance of public opinion, and means of redress, or even punishment, of the violations committed.

Professor Cassin's emphasis on the concept of man as a community and man as an individual; his classification of rights according to the ideas of liberty, equality and security; the principles of the unity of the human race and of the equality of men; the fundamental importance of the protection of human life; and his emphasis on measures of implementation would later test the United Nations and its organs including the Security Council.

How did the Security Council stand up to this test? Its early record was not particularly stellar and has been traced by Sydney Bailey in his work on the Security Council and the Protection of Human Rights. In the years since the end of the Cold War, the Security Council's record has improved markedly to the extent that leading commentators on the Charter of the United Nations are now able to assert that the Security Council could become active in cases of human rights violations without first determining the existence of a threat to the peace in the sense of Chapter 7 of the Charter. This is the view enunciated in the commentary on the Charter of the United Nations edited by Professor Simma. We look briefly at this next.

III. Legal Foundations

The competence of the Security Council to deal with gross violations of human rights has gained growing acceptance through practice. The Commentary on the Charter of the United Nations edited by Bruno Simma recognized this thus:

> In later years, a question that gained importance in the practice of the Security Council was whether the Security Council could concern itself with human rights violations, a problem which was already touched upon in the debate on the Spanish question. This question was discussed in the case of Angola and with regard to the situation in Southern Africa, namely the South African apartheid regime. In the course of these discussions, the decisions on whether the Security Council could become active in cases of human rights violations without first determining the existence of a threat to the peace in the sense of Chapter VII of the Charter, and specifically on whether it could exercise powers that went beyond those enumerated in Art. 24(2), second sentence, was again left open, because with increasingly strong argumentation the Security Council has qualified gross violations of human rights as constituting a threat to the peace in the sense of the Charter. In the course of these discussions, it also became clear that the position taken in the Spanish and the Trieste Cases, according to which the Security Council was considered to possess the necessary powers under Art. 24(1) to fulfil its tasks in the maintenance of peace beyond the enumeration in Art. 24(2) second sentence, was still accepted. This position of the Security Council was corroborated by the *Namibia* advisory opinion of the International Court of Justice.[9]

In a recent work we have reviewed the practice of the Security Council and concluded that the role of the Security Council in the protection of human rights has become even more explicit in its contemporary practice.[10]

IV. Policy Framework

A. The Legislative and Normative Principle: The practice of the Council is replete with examples of resolutions and decisions in which it has placed its authority behind the corpus of human rights and humanitarian law. From this one can conclude that the norms of international human rights and humanitarian law are an integral part of the legisla-

---

9. B. Simma (Ed.), Commentary on the Charter of the United Nations (1995), p.406.
10. B.G. Ramcharan, The Security Council and the Protection of Human Rights. Kluwer Law International (2002).

tive, policy and intellectual framework of the Security Council as it grapples with issues of international peace and security.

B. The Principle of Democratic Legitimacy: It is possible to deduce from the recent practice of the Security Council the principle of democratic legitimacy, namely, that governments should be based on popular consent, the rule of law and respect for human rights, and that governments freely elected and faithful to the mandate given them by the people, should not be violently overthrown. In the case of Sierra Leone for example, the Security Council gave voice to this principle consistently.

C. The Principle of Justice: The Security Council's establishment of international tribunals to deal with allegations of war crimes and crimes against humanity in the former Yugoslavia and in Rwanda provide the basis for postulating the principle of justice, namely that the Security Council is prepared at times to provide legal sanction against those accused of grave breaches of international human rights and humanitarian law.

D. The Principle of Respect for Human Rights and Humanitarian Law during conflicts: There are numerous examples in which the Security Council has called on parties to conflict to respect international human rights norms and norms of humanitarian law.

E. The Conflict Prevention Principle: The Security Council is gradually developing a practice of being briefed on developments in the human rights area. One can postulate an emerging principle of attentiveness to human rights indicators for purposes of early warning and conflict prevention.

F. The Peace-making Principle: One can deduce from the practice of the Security Council in evaluating the work of peace negotiators in particular conflicts the principle that in the drafting of peace agreements every effort should be made to incorporate into them solid regimes for the promotion and protection of human rights in the future.

G. The Peace-keeping Principle: Increasingly, as the Security Council establishes United Nations peace-keeping and observer operations, it endows them with a human rights component.

H. The Peace-building Principle: Human rights are increasingly integrated in peace-building activities.

I. The Protection Principle: The Security Council's establishment of safe havens and safe areas provide the basis for postulating the protection principle. However, the Council has found it easier to legislate than to enforce.

J. The Confidence-Building Principle: While seeking to take account of the preceding principles, one should never lose sight of the fact that the Security Council is an organ that, by the very nature of its mandate, needs to strive for pragmatic compromises. At times therefore it will, perforce, be called upon to apply the confidence-building principle; that is to say that the Council must work together with those in a position to bring conflicts to an end through pragmatic approaches.

K. The Political Principle: Flowing from the confidence-building principle is the political principle namely that as the organ that theoretically groups the most powerful nations in the world, it is unavoidable that they will often be moved by political considerations. The political principle is inherent in the nature of the Security Council and is probably crucial to its overall success. One should therefore never lose sight of it.

L. The Power Principle: Closely related to the political principle is the power factor: namely that on occasions the overwhelming power of some of its members will, unfortunately, be applied in ways that are at variance with the human rights and justice principles. That, alas, is a reality of the international order at the start of the twenty-first century.

Despite these constraints, we believe that it is possible to distill an emerging protection concept in the Security Council which we set out next.

V. Principles for dealing with human rights situations impacting on international peace and security

The practice of the Council suggests that the following principles have influenced the Council in addressing human rights situations.

a. Threat to international peace and security

On 9 November 1996, the Security Council determined 'that the magnitude of the present humanitarian crisis in eastern Zaire constitutes a threat to international peace and security in the region.'[11]

b. The integration of human rights in conflict resolution

In a Presidential statement on Georgia, the Security Council expressed 'its support for the Secretary-General's efforts to find ways of improving the observance of human rights in the region as an integral part of the work

11. S/RES/1078 (1996), 9 November, 1996.

towards a comprehensive settlement.'[12] In a similar statement on Liberia, the Security Council stressed 'the importance of respect for human rights in Liberia.'[13] In a similar resolution on Liberia, the Council urged "all Liberian parties to cooperate with the peace process, including by respecting human rights and facilitating humanitarian activities and disarmament."The Council stressed 'the importance of respect for human rights in Liberia, not least in the period leading up to elections, and emphasizes the human rights aspect of the mandate of UNOMIL.'[14]

In resolution 1217 (1998) of 22 December 1998 on Cyprus, the Council reaffirmed its position that a settlement must be based on a State of Cyprus with a single sovereignty and international personality and a single citizenship, with its independence and territorial integrity safeguarded, and comprising two politically equal communities as described in the relevant Security Council resolutions, in a bi-communal and bi-zonal federation, and that such a settlement must exclude union in whole or in part with any other country or any form of partition or secession.

c. Democratic legitimacy

In a Presidential Statement on Burundi, the Security Council declared its grave concern 'at recent information on political developments in Burundi. It strongly condemns any attempt to overthrow the present legitimate Government by force or coup d'etat.'[15] Likewise, in a resolution on Liberia, the Council expressed 'its support for the resolve of the ECOWAS Ministers not to recognize any Government in Liberia that comes to office through the use of force.'[16] In the same vein, the Council 'emphasized that the holding of free and fair elections as scheduled is an essential phase of the peace process in Liberia.'[17]

In the case of Sierra Leone, the Council affirmed that it would 'continue to support the development of peace and democracy in Sierra Leone.'[18]

---

12. S/PRST/1996/20:The situation in Georgia.
13. S/RES/1059 (1996), 31 May 1996
14. Resolution 1100 (1997), Liberia.
15. S/PRST/1996/31, 24 July, 1996.
16. S/RES/1059, 31 May, 1996.
17. Resolution 1100 (1997): Liberia
18. S/PV.3720, Sierra Leone (4 December, 1996)

d. The highest standards of human rights

The Council has, on various occasions, expressly come out in favour of the highest standards of human rights. In a 1996 resolution on Croatia, it reaffirmed 'the importance of full compliance by the parties with their commitments as specified in the Basic Agreement to respect the highest standards of human rights and fundamental freedoms and to promote an atmosphere of confidence among all local residents irrespective of their ethnic origin, and, in this context, urges the Government of the Republic of Croatia to ensure respect for the rights of all national ethnic groups.'[19]

e. The Rights of Women

On 28 August 1998, the Council, deeply concerned at the continuing discrimination against girls and women and at other violations of human rights and of international humanitarian law in Afghanistan, reaffirmed that all parties to the conflict were bound to comply with their obligations under international humanitarian law and in particular the Geneva Conventions of 12 August 1949, and that persons who committed or ordered the commission of grave breaches of the Conventions were individually responsible in respect of such breaches. The Council urged the Afghan factions to put an end to the discrimination against girls and women and to other violations of human rights as well as violations of international humanitarian law and to adhere to the internationally accepted norms and standards in this sphere.[20]

f. International humanitarian law

The Council has on many occasions underlined 'the obligation of all concerned strictly to respect the relevant provisions of international humanitarian law.'[21] The Security Council has consistently called upon all parties to the conflict and all others concerned to respect strictly the provisions of international humanitarian law. For example, the Council has 'stressed the importance of respect for human rights in Liberia as well as the need to rehabilitate promptly the penitentiary system in this country.'

In resolution 1216 (1998) of 21 December 1998, the Council called upon all concerned, including the Government and the self-proclaimed military junta to respect strictly relevant provisions of international law, including

---

19. Resolution 1079 (1996), Croatia.

20. S/RES/1193, 28 August 1998.

21. Resolution 1080 (1996), on the Great Lakes region of Africa.

humanitarian and human rights law, and to ensure safe and unimpeded access by international humanitarian organizations to persons in need of assistance as a result of the conflict.

g. The duty of the State

In a Presidential Statement on the protection of UN personnel, the Council underlined that '...the host country and others concerned must take all appropriate steps to ensure the safety and security of United Nations personnel and premises.'[22]

h. The duty of all concerned

In a Presidential Statement on Albania, the Council appealed 'to all concerned to refrain from the use of violence and to respect the legitimate institutions and to reach a peaceful solution to the crisis on the basis of democratic principles.' It called upon the parties involved 'to continue the political dialogue...and to live up the commitment undertaken' and urged that all political forces responsibly cooperate, in view of lowering tensions and facilitate the stabilization of the country.[23]

i. Non-use of violence

In a Presidential Statement on the then Zaire, the Council declared that it was 'gravely concerned at the deteriorating situation in the Great Lakes region, in particular eastern Zaire, and at the effect which the continued fighting is having on the inhabitants of the region and condemns all acts of violence. It underlines the urgent need for a comprehensive and coordinated response by the international community to prevent any further escalation of the crisis there.'[24] In one resolution it reiterated 'its condemnation of all acts of violence, and its call for an immediate cease-fire and a complete cessation of all hostilities in the region.'[25] In another resolution on Albania, the Council condemned 'all acts of violence and calls for their immediate end.'[26] Likewise in another resolution, the Council condemned 'all acts of violence and calls

---

22. S/PRST/1997/13 : Use of force against United Nations personnel.
23. S/PRST/1997/14 : Albania
24. S/PRST/1996/44, 1 October 1996.
25. Resolution 1080 (1996), Great Lakes
26. Resolution 1101 (1997), Albania

for an immediate cease-fire and a complete cessation of all hostilities in the region.'[27]

j. Impunity

In a communication to the Secretary-General on Burundi, the members of the Security Council stated their belief that it was 'vital that measures to deal with the problem of impunity should be addressed in the context of a negotiated political settlement in Burundi.'[28]

k. Minority rights

In a Presidential Statement of 3 July 1996, the Council said it was 'deeply concerned at the failure by the Croatian Government to take sufficient measures to safeguard the rights of the local Serb population and to ensure their safety and well-being. The Council is also deeply concerned at the Croatian Government's failure to promote conditions, including satisfactory procedures, facilitating the return of all Croatian Serbs who wish to do so. The Council strongly deplores such failure to act.'

The Council noted that 'the Croatian Government has begun to cooperate with international human rights mechanisms, and that it has considered various initiatives for the protection of minority rights. Nevertheless the Council underlines that the Croatian Government must undertake determined and sustained efforts to ensure respect for the protection of the rights of Croatian Serbs and to provide for their safeguarding in the legal and constitutional framework of the Republic of Croatia, including by the reactivation of the relevant articles of its Constitutional Law. The Council reminds the Croatian Government that its obligation to promote respect for, and protection of, such rights cannot be made conditional upon other factors, including upon political negotiations with the Federal Republic of Yugoslavia.'[29]

VI. Principles for Humanitarian Intercession

The practice of the Security Council indicates that it may review any situation from the point of view of the maintenance of international peace and security; it may also investigate any situation from point of view of maintenance of

---

27. S/RES/1078 (1996), 9 November 1996.
28. Letter of 24 September 1996 to the Secretary-General on Burundi.
29. S/PRST/1996/29, 3 July, 1996.

international peace and security. The Security Council may intercede if:

a. The situation involves a breach of international peace and security. (Powers under the Charter.)

In relation to the then Zaire: the Council determined that 'the magnitude of the present humanitarian crisis in eastern Zaire constitutes a threat to international peace and security in the region.'[30]

b. The humanitarian situation is of such magnitude as to warrant intervention.

In relation to the situation in Somalia, the Indian representative in the Security Council articulated the principle that: 'The sheer magnitude of the problem and its continuation constitute a threat to the peace and security of the region. The Somali situation is thus *sui generis* and... has eluded conventional solutions....'[31]

c. The Government requests

It is clear that if the government concerned requests, the Council can respond.

d. The situation involves a breakdown of governmental authority

If there is a total breakdown of government authority, as in Somalia, the Council can clearly act.

e. The situation involves an international crime, e.g. apartheid

The Security Council vigorously condemned the Apartheid system on many occasions.

f. The situation involves terrorism

The Council is on record as having condemned terrorism in general and in particular situations.

g. The situation involves gross violations of international humanitarian and human rights law

On 15 September 1999, in resolution 1264, the Council expressed 'its concern at reports indicating that systematic, widespread and flagrant violations of international humanitarian and human rights law have been committed in East Timor', and stressed 'that persons committing such violations bear indi-

30. S/RES/1078 (1996), 9 November 1996.
31. S/PV.3060, pp.31-32.

vidual responsibility.'

h. *The situation involves the protection of humanitarian convoys*

In relation to the conflict in Bosnia, the Council acted repeatedly for the protection of humanitarian convoys.

i. *The situation involves the protection of civilians in armed conflict*

On 19 February 1992, the Security Council expressed its deep concern about the renewed and rising cycle of violence in southern Lebanon and elsewhere in the Middle East. The Council statement read in part as follows:

> The members of the Council are deeply concerned about the renewed and rising cycle of violence in southern Lebanon and elsewhere in the region. The Council deplores in particular the recent killings and the continued violence which threatens to claim additional lives and to destabilize the region further. The members of the Council call upon all those involved to exercise maximum restraint in order to bring such violence to an end.

In a 1998 Presidential Statement on Angola, the Security Council expressed 'its deep concern at the worsening humanitarian situation in Angola' and emphasized the responsibility of the Government of Angola and the leadership of UNITA to facilitate humanitarian assistance efforts, guarantee the safety and freedom of movement of humanitarian workers and permit an independent assessment of the needs of the civilian population, to be carried out swiftly in any part of the country as necessary. The Council also expressed concern at the plight of those most vulnerable groups, such as children, women, the elderly and internally displaced persons who are particularly at risk and need special protection. The Council urged the Government of Angola and the leadership of UNITA to ensure full respect for international humanitarian, refugee and human rights law.[32]

In another 1999 Presidential Statement on Angola, the Council expressed its profound concern at the humanitarian impact of the conflict on the Angolan people. It urges the international community to support the Government of Angola in fulfilling its primary responsibility for the humanitarian needs of the Angolan people and, in this regard, urged Member States to fund generously the 1999 Consolidated Humanitarian Appeal for Angola. It called upon all

32. S/PRST/1998/37

concerned to concur and cooperate with United Nations humanitarian assistance activities on the basis of the principles of neutrality and non-discrimination, to guarantee the security and freedom of movement of humanitarian personnel, and to ensure necessary, adequate and safe access and logistics by land and air. It urged all concerned to cooperate with the human rights activities of the United Nations, which help to lay a basis for lasting peace and national reconciliation.[33]

On 17 September 1999, dealing with the protection of civilians in armed conflict, the Council expressed 'its willingness to respond to situations of armed conflict where civilians are being targeted or humanitarian assistance to civilians is being deliberately obstructed, including through the consideration of appropriate measures at the Council's disposal in accordance with the Charter of the United Nations, and notes, in that regard, the relevant recommendations contained in the report of the Secretary-General.'

The practice of the Council is evolving significantly with regard, for example, to its unequivocal condemnation of terrorism and its establishment of international tribunals for dealing with grave breaches of international humanitarian and human rights law. The concept of security is also evolving in the Council as it has sought to grapple with issues such as HIV/AIDS, the protection of civilians, and the rights of women. The Council has also sought in recent years to integrate human rights into efforts for conflict prevention, peace-making, peace-keeping, and peace-building. All of this demonstrates that, through practice, the Council's work is taking on a significant human rights dimension, within the framework of its responsibilities for the maintenance of international peace and security in accordance with the United Nations Charter.

VII. The Emerging Protection Concept

From the recent practice of the Security Council, it could be concluded that the human rights ethic has entered the Security Council in a significant way even if it is not predominant. Perhaps the strongest strand in the practice of the Council relates to justice and accountability in the face of gross violations of human rights.

The practice of the Security Council suggests that it could become engaged in human rights situations such as the following:

---

33. S/PRST/1999/3

- those which entail threats to, or breaches of, international peace and security;
- those which involve a breakdown of governmental authority in the country concerned;
- those which entail a flouting of the authority of the United Nations;
- those which involve a high magnitude of human suffering or crimes against humanity;
- where the government so requests;
- where the conscience of the international community is shocked.

The Security Council's composition and characteristics are such that it is unlikely to become engaged in situations involving one of its Permanent Members. At least one of the Permanent Members is known to take a conservative approach to the Council's role in dealing with human rights issues—even if it has demonstrated a great deal of flexibility in practice.

It would be wise to expect incremental developments in the role of the Security Council in dealing with gross human rights violations rather than quantum leaps. The Security Council is not meant to duplicate the role of the human rights organs, nor to supplant them. It is meant to complement and support them and to take action in situations where the exercise of its authority could bring protection to those at risk—such as the deployment of preventive peace-keepers or observers or the deployment of protection forces.

Perhaps the most important thing the human rights community could do would be to make sure that Members of the Security Council are kept abreast of the trends and currents on human rights and, in particular, that the Council is briefed about the human rights dimensions of situations on its agenda. The work of the thematic and country rapporteurs of the Commission on Human Rights comes to mind particularly in this regard.

From the practice of the Security Council, the following strands of the emerging protection concept could be identified for future application and development:

i. the deployment of preventive peace-keepers or observers for protection purposes;
ii. the insistence on negotiated solutions and national dialogue in dealing with internal conflicts;
iii. emphasis on democracy, the rule of law, and respect for human rights in negotiating solutions to internal conflicts;
iv. the call for justice for the victims of gross violations of human rights;

v. the establishment of human rights components in peace-keeping operations;
vi. the inclusion of human rights mandates in peace-building operations;
vii. the designation of protected and safe areas—provided they are backed up;
viii. the establishment of protection forces;
ix. support for the International Criminal Court;
x. support for nationally-established courts such as that which the Security Council called for in Sierra Leone;
xi. focusing on groups at risk such as children, women, and HIV/AIDS victims;
xii. showing a human face, where called for, in the imposition of sanctions;
xiii. continued adoption of resolutions and Presidential statements that bring the Council in line with the conscience of the international community;
xiv. listening to the voices of the human rights movement and taking their information and insights into account in its work;
xv. being a strong agent of human rights protection where people are at risk and use of the authority of the Security Council is called for.

Conclusion

A Security Council that is moved by considerations of justice and by a willingness to act for the protection of those at risk will be faithful to the Charter's vision of peace grounded in economic and social justice and respect for human rights. This is the path that the Peoples of the United Nations expect the Security Council to walk in the future.

The Future Shape of Europe

Robert Badinter*

I. Drafting a European Constitution

We are now in an extraordinary political process regarding the drafting of a constitution for Europe. This was a very unusual method. Constitutions are normally drafted in a constitutional assembly by deputies, who have been appointed by their constituencies to draft a project. Sometimes they adopt the project directly, and at other times offer it up for the approval of citizens via referendum. They have a special mandate to draft a constitution and have been elected for that purpose.

When this type of procedure is adopted, as with all debating assemblies, you have different factions, left and right, conservative and progressive, in confrontation. A majority arises and you come to a result. What happened in Brussels is different. In this respect, the use of the word convention is a little deceptive. It is more or less a commission of very capable people from the European Commission committed by their own governments, ministers of foreign affairs and members of national and European parliaments. We do not

* Former French Minister of Justice, Senator, Member of the European Convention. Lecture delivered to a joint meeting of CCJO and the Anglo-Jewish association on 10 March 2003.

Raphael Walden (ed.), Racism and Human Rights, *31-39.*

vote. We try to reach consensus, a term which implies significantly that you are not a gentleman if you dissent. It does not allow a majority vote, but rather aristocratic behaviour from the leading parts of the convention and the presidium, which is composed of about 10 people and led by former Prime Minister Amato and the Former Prime Minister Doué.

As things are, one positive result is certain: we shall come out with a proposed draft of a constitution. However, we must considering the method, and remember that this constitution, by a unique phenomenon, will be adopted in a treaty with all that engenders regarding its ratification. It is not executed by a deliberative assembly, but by a mixture of technical advisors, commissioners and political negotiators.

I feel we are in the negotiation of an international treaty, rather than in the deliberation of a constitution. I should stress that this process is not only for methodological purposes, but also because the approach is different. When you draft a constitution you start from principles and then propose a rational project. When you enter an international negotiation it is a process of give and take; there is a permanent exchange going on. This opens the way to a final result, which may have some marks of its origin. It will be a constitution, but at the same time also the result of a negotiation.

I would say bluntly that good constitutions are like the machines of the 18th century: those beautiful things, which were crafted at the time with checks and balances so that they worked. Now we would have a gas factory rather than a machine: something that would be very strange and which we would have to adopt or refuse.

II. Principles of a Constitution

Now is a good time to appreciate the situation, to ascertain what has been accepted by almost everybody by consensus, and to look at the problems ahead, which are much more important than what has already been effected. What has already been brought about? First, the principle of a constitution.

In a contemporary context a constitution necessarily has three levels. First is a bill of rights, une déclaration des droits fundamentaux, because you have to stress the values for which we stand. Then, more seldom but nevertheless present in contemporary constitutions, there is *l'état des droits*, the system of rights, which guarantees to the citizen that they will have the right to have the constitution respected. This part contains the legal instrument, the hierarchy of norms and, most importantly, the judiciary, which will allow the rights in the constitution to be protected against the other powers.

We have made great progress in the system of rights. We have agreed that the treaties will be merged into the new constitution. There will be one instrument, unlike the way things work now. The pillars and their many complexities will disappear. However, this does not mean that there will be different procedures, especially in terms of the voting process, in different fields of interest. The union will have recognition of its international personality and will therefore be able to ratify international treaties, particularly the European Convention on Human Rights. In so far as guarantees can be provided for the citizen, we are working now to improve the access to the Court of Justice in Luxembourg.

There is essential technical legal work carrying on. At the moment we have thirteen types of norms, which can be rendered and adopted by the Union and which will be percolated to five clear and constant factors.

III. The Constitution and National Sovereignty

In any constitution, once you have mentioned the bill of rights and the guarantee of the state of law, there remains the essential point: where is the main subject, power? This refers to the institutions themselves and the mechanisms that make them work. I come here to the core of the subject. In order to clarify it, because it is so unique in the history of constitution drafting, one must remember that traditionally constitutions are the expression of sovereignty. By changing the sovereignty one transfers it through evolution from the king to the people. You need a constitution. If you rise up to independence, as in the post-colonial period, you of course start by drafting your constitution.

1. Sources of Sovereignty

Here it is different. The Union proceeds from two sources of sovereignty, which are to be combined in one constitution. This is a unique situation. The two sources include, first of all, the delegation of sovereignty by states. Remember that states will remain sovereign whatever the constitution of the Union. We are not elaborating a federal constitution, as was the case in 1787: *c'est ne pas un état fédérale*. It is a union of sovereign states. Even if one uses the term 'federation of sovereign states' they are still sovereign, which has many consequences, notably in the field of international relations, as seen today.

Apart from this delegation of sovereignty that is transferred by the states to the Union, the most remarkable case being the states that belong to the Euro, there is another source of sovereignty, less well perceived by the people. This source comes from the community, which, once the ratification occurs, will consist of more than 450 million people. These are citizens of their own states and will keep their nationality. However, one must remember that after Maastricht each of us is an English or French citizen as well as a citizen of the Union. This means that there is a community of 450 million, soon to include 25-27 states. The expression of the general will of this community, which is unique in history, is of course the European Parliament. This parliament is, per se, not a national parliament, nor is it a conjunction of representatives of their own parliaments. Rather, it is the expression of this 450-million-strong community of European people. In addition, as typical of the interest of the community, you also have the Commission.

IV. Institutional Developments within the European Union

As things are, it has been decided that the so-called 'triangle of institutions' will not change. In other terms, we shall try not to bring any new institutions into the frame. As you will recall, two tendencies are sharing the stage. The division inside of the Convention does not pass through traditional left-right lines of political parties. Rather, there is a more communitarian approach. The other trend relates to the ones who want to keep power more on the other line: state sovereignty versus federalism. These are the two trends visible in the Convention. Considering this, you can see where we can come to a form of synthesis, as well as what type of solution is appearing at present.

1. The European Commission

On the side of the Union, including the institutions of the Commission and the European Parliament, progress is made in an extension of power. In order to govern such a large ensemble of states, comprising of 450 million people across some 25-27 states, you need a very strong Commission, without which we will go nowhere and will be unable to handle the task of governance. Hence, everybody agrees that the Commission should remain strong.

Problems include agreement on the composition of the Commission. Each state will have one commissioner. The new member states desperately want this. This will mean reorganisation of the Commission, since having 25 people necessitates a reorganisation of the structure. With a competent three or four, working in the same field and with one Vice-President, it will not raise any technical problems. The question that is now being thoroughly discussed is that of the presidency of the Commission.

There are two versions as to why this is so. The first states that we should keep the present line as it is, with only slight modifications. The President of the Commission, an extraordinarily important personality considering the reinforcement of the Commission, will be chosen, through a qualified majority vote, by the European Council. The Council, which consists of heads of states and governments, will choose the President of the Commission, and the European Parliament will give its approval. This is a more technical approach, which in fact gives more power to the heads of state and government.

The other approach, which is the one of the Commission, the Parliament and the Franco-German proposal, says 'no'. The President of the Commission should be appointed first by the Parliament. The system is such that after the election of the European Parliament there would necessarily be a majority and a minority. The majority of the European Parliament will then appoint the President of the Commission, who will subsequently have to be approved by the European Council for heads of government. He will then choose the members of the Commission, and they will all return as a team before the European Parliament. It is a system in which one must realise that we go through a parliamentary system of managing the European Union. This is because a majority choosing from within its ranks the leader of the executive is no different from the ordinary system with a majority and a Prime Minister.

I must stress that this is the type of institution that is common in Europe. It has major importance in terms of politics, in the sense that if, following an election from all the people of Europe, the majority of the Parliament chooses one candidate to be the President of the Commission, it is politically speaking impossible that the heads of government disagree with the choice made. It would be a major crisis in Europe, with the Council confronted about how they dare to challenge the will of the majority elected by the people. This means that the President of the Commission will in fact politically be chosen by the Parliament.

These are the two versions, which are nowadays in confrontation with one another. The European Parliament will no doubt have its powers increased, such as by having proceedings by co-decision as the rule for all laws to be adopted in the new system. Also, apart from the designation of the President of the Commission and the responsibility of the Commission before the

Parliament, the Parliament will probably have a greater and stronger part in determining the European taxes that will come into the budget. Parliament will decide not only the expenses, but also part of the receipts.

2. The European Council

Looking towards the other source of sovereignty, there are also certain conclusions to be drawn. It can be foreseen that the European Council as such will preside over the formal authority that will decide over the main choices of the Union. As an example, the question of Turkey will be decided by the European Council in the first instance. There is an essential question pertaining to minority and majority issues, as well as to proceedings of decisions. Will the European Council decide on all matters at the qualified majority in major instances, or will it keep people speaking immediately for some fields, such as European international politics and security policies? This is in discussion, and the present situation naturally makes it far more difficult than it was.

Apart from the European Council, which keeps its part in terms of fundamental decisions, there is the Council of Ministers. It will act as all other legislative bodies. Remember that it is composed of representatives of member states, and will play the part of a second chamber for the laws. This is no doubt a federal approach in the sense that they will have to decide whether or not to accept the drafts proposed by the Commission and voted on by the Parliament. Apart from that, the Council of Ministers will of course have an executive delegation from the European Council in order to decide on the various aspects in relation to the political choices decided upon by the European Parliament.

3. The Presidency of the European Union

In considering the system, one sees that it is more or less difficult to handle. There is at present one burning question, on which I shall bring forward both criticism and a suggestion, namely the question of the presidency of the Union. Under the present system a new member state takes up the presidency every six months, in a rotating order decided by the calendar. Six months is a very short period of time, and reflects the fact that the system was designed for a Union of six states, for which it worked well. Then Union then grew, first to 12 member states and then to 15. At 25 member states it would mean that every 12 years the presidency would come back to a member state. Some small states and, more significantly, all new members of the Union definitely want to keep the system.

Technically speaking, the system is very bad. Changing the presidency every six months is akin to the king moving from one castle to the other, having to bring all the documents and dossiers and get ready; it is a waste of time. Furthermore, the citizens of Europe do not understand the system. It is anonymous, as becomes clear if one asks any fellow citizen which country currently has the presidency of the Union, and which country will be in charge in another six months' time.

Still, the presidency satisfies the pride of nationalism. In this context the East is very interesting. One must realise that the new members are coming out from the darkness of history and have suffered. They have long been subject to the history of major empires, by which they have been crushed or divided. For most of them, they have for the last 50 years been under the full control of a major imperialist power, the Soviet Union. Now, for the first time for some of them, they come out into history and are sovereign. To realise what this means, let us take the example of Lithuania. To be President of the European Union would be a source of genuine recognition and dignity as well as proof of equality among all members of the Union. It is thus easy to understand why they want this. Still, it does not change the fact that this is a very bad way.

The proposal that was made was called ABC, referring to Aznar, Blair and Chirac. As divorce has occurred since, the phrase ABC cannot be used for the proposal. The current proposal is a Franco-German one under which the President of the European Council should be personally appointed for five years and chosen by the European Council among their peers. As such, it will mean a former president or prime minister. He or she will preside over the European Council and represent the Union as such for five years on the external seat, taking care mostly of the external problems. This system not only grieves members from Eastern Europe and worries small states, which have produced many a great statesman in the Union; it also cannot work in my opinion. The legitimacy of the presidency of the Union comes from one source, namely the Parliament. The legitimacy of the presidency of the European Council will come directly from the states. One will be the expression of the people, the other the expression of the sources. The two legitimacies will each have a presidency, with no second-rate personalities. None of them will have any possibility of challenging the other, wherefore we are in a situation that in France is called cohabitation. It is a cohabitation between the President of the Commission and the President of the European Council, with no way to solve it.

Furthermore, the French-German proposition said that the President of the European Council will mostly deal with external affairs, while the other will take care of internal affairs. It is already difficult in the context of a national state, as seen in France, and it will be impossible when it comes to the Union. The reason for this is that most of the affairs of the European Union have an international dimension, whether one speaks of foreign policy, environmental protection, agricultural interest or external commercial trade. You will therefore have the two of them with power on the same field of competency, which cannot work. It will necessarily hamper the dynamics and bring into the Union a source of conflict.

V. Conclusions

For this reason one must go back to reality, which in today's modern politics is that the European people, like others, only believe in what they watch on TV. As mentioned, Europe has up until now been just a concept. People do not see Europe. When President Chirac was presiding over the European Council in Nice no one saw in him anyone other than the President of the French Republic. No one thought he was the President of the European Union. We therefore need to go back to the fundamentals. Firstly, we must have a President of the Union. Secondly, we must remember that the Union is not an ensemble created to make business only. The Union stands because the people of Europe share the same fundamental values. They have a common history and culture as well as common fundamental values. If they depart from that there will be no more European Union. Therefore, there should be appointed as President of the European Union a charismatic personality with a significant moral role rather than a political one. It should embody an expression of the Union and be a permanent presence that would remind the Union what it stands for.

I must remind you that the poisons, such as wild nationalism, xenophobia, racism and anti-Semitism, which have so deeply altered European history, have not vanished from Europe and are always ready to show up again. It is necessary, in times of crisis, to have a voice within the European Union that challenges these poisons. To give you an example from recent constitutional history, Germany in 1945 did not know where it stood. It wanted to be a democracy, but it did not know what it was anymore, considering recent history. The thinking, along with a very strong intuition, made them feel what the philosopher Habermas has rightly called 'constitutional patriotism'. Germany could be rebuilt only based on the fundamental values of democracy.

The President was there to remind Germans, if necessary, on what values New Germany was founded, and why the constitution, as the ultimate expression and granter, was a necessity for Germany to avoid it going back to its poisons. It should be the same for the Union. It is the time for bringing up someone as a President of the European Union, chosen by the European Council, but appointed by the European Parliament. No political role, other than as chairman of the European Council every six months, but a moral role, which is very important for the future of the European Union. This is the proposal I stand for. We shall see what will come out of this very difficult problem.

Slavery as Piracy—The Legal Case for Reparations for Slavery

Geraldine Van Bueren*

The Need for a Bold, Just and Consistent Approach

The purpose of reparations is the restoration of dignity: the dignity of survivors, the dignity of the memory of the dead and the dignity achieved by making restitution for past wrongs. The very act of restoration provides all parties with the feeling of dignity. This is the ethos and the building of a global community framework in which reparations for slavery ought to be discussed. It is the spirit in which the question, whether present generations should pay for the crimes of their ancestors and others to whom they are unrelated, should be answered.

A state commits an internationally wrongful act when it is in violation of an applicable rule of international law; either treaty or customary law. Most

---

* Barrister, Professor of International Human Rights Law at Queen Mary, University of London and WP Schreiner Professor, Faculty of Law, University of Cape Town. This is an extended version of a commissioned paper for the United Nations Durban Conference on Racism which has also appeared in a collection of papers edited by C van der Anker. I am grateful to the Consultative Council of Jewish Organisations for their support.

Raphael Walden (ed.), Racism and Human Rights, *41-53.*

of the international laws cited in support of a slavery reparations claim are twentieth-century developments drafted and adopted after the cessation of the majority of slavery. It is difficult therefore to argue that they should be applied retrospectively when this was clearly not the intent lying behind the laws. Yet there are international laws which could succeed but which have not been used. First it is necessary to distinguish between slavery and the slave trade. Secondly it is necessary to reconceptualise the slave trade as a form of piracy and piracy has been illegal for centuries. There is historical evidence to support this approach.

Any legal claim for reparations for slavery must be based on the enduring consequences of the legacy of slavery which continues to affect those living today. If it is argued that the period of time which has passed since African slavery is not critical why exclude other historical acts of slavery. As valid as the claim for reparations is, from Africa and descendants of those who once lived in Africa, it is not the continent which is the salient factor but the slavery. Reparations should not necessarily be limited to the descendants of those enslaved in one continent or the descendants from that continent. Any claim for reparations for slavery, unless waived, ought to include the other continuing traces of slavery. What for example distinguishes African slavery from the slavery in South America?

Reparations should be seen as a part of the honest acceptance of the past and of accepting moral and legal responsibility. Within this lens compensation does not have to be considered within a narrow context. The discussions surrounding debt relief take on a completely different hue. In the past the linking of debt relief to poverty reduction has erroneously often been perceived as special pleading by African states. Arguably some of the debts owe their origin to remedying an impoverishment to which slavery may have contributed. The carefully targeted cancellation of this debt is therefore not an issue only of relief but becomes a facet of compensation and therefore of justice.

Similarly the targetted liberalisation of trade and the removal of trade barriers from the states from which slaves were trafficked could also be considered within the context of reparations.

Reparation is a form of restitution: the return of unjust enrichment at the expense of others. It is not necessarily prompted by individual guilt. Guilt and shame have to be distinguished. Guilt is an immobilising emotion allowing individuals the luxury of feeling bad but doing nothing; shame is not and need not be related to feelings of individual responsibility.

The claim for reparations is growing.[1] We should recognise that a bolder approach is needed. After all it was a new and bold approach which led to the development of the regional and international human rights system. Less than a century ago the violation of human rights behind a nation's borders remained principally that state's exclusive concern.[2] We forget how new it was to place the individual at the centre of a system prior to the development of international human rights law and the extent of the resistance. When the Nuremberg Tribunal was held it was criticised by many, including by international lawyers. However, 'whatever the state of the law in 1945, Article 6 of the Nuremberg Charter has since come to represent general international law.'[3] In other words what was once considered an innovative mechanism issuing groundbreaking jurisprudence has now been resited in the acceptable. The Nuremberg Tribunal provides a lesson but it is not a parallel. The lesson is that reparation and accountability can be reconceptualised within a larger global justice framework and still justice can be attained. This is a call for an international charter for slavery reparations.

Of Piracy and the Slave Trade

The most common legal examples cited in support of a claim for reparations for slavery do not suffice as legal precedents. The cases frequently cited are the judgement of the Nuremberg Tribunal and the subsequent reparations for the Holocaust; the United Nations Genocide Convention 1948 and the damages paid to indigenous peoples, including Maoris, for violations by non-indigenous settlers.

Admittedly it is true that there are many similarities between slavery in Africa and Latin America and the German slavery and attempted extermination of the Jews. The dominant regimes characterised both groups as racially

---

1. See for example, Dolgopol and Paranjape, *Comfort Women: An Unfinished Ordeal*, 1994. Korean women who were used as sexual slaves by Japan.
2. 'States were obliged to abstain from interfering in the internal affairs of one another. International law was not concerned with way in which a state treated its own nationals in its own territory. It is a cliche of modern international law that the classical theory no longer prevails in its unadulterated form.' *Millet L in R* v. *Bow Street Metropolitan Stipendiary Magistrate ex parte Pinochet Ugarte* (Amnesty International and Other Intervening) (No 3) 2 All E.R.97, 170 1999.
3. Brownlie, Principles of Public International Law, 1990 at 562.

inferior. It is also true that both the Holocaust and the slave trade transported people in degrading and inhuman conditions across geographic borders: Jews were transported across Europe and the slave traders transported out of Africa. However, on closer examination there are important legal differences between these claims and the claim for reparations for slavery.

The key issue is whether at the time of the commission of the slavery it was an illegal act either under domestic law or under international law. The Nuremberg judgement and the payment to indigenous peoples have been on the basis that there was a violation of law at the time of the commission of the offences.

Article 6 of the Charter of the Nuremberg Tribunal[4] included within its definition of crimes against humanity 'enslavement, deportation'.[5] It is clear that slavery falls well within these definitions. This is unarguable. However, a careful reading of the judgement of Nuremberg shows that the Tribunal held that many of the crimes committed against the Jews within Germany before the War, as 'revolting and horrible as many of these crimes were' not established as being committed 'in execution of, or in connection with' any crime within the Tribunal's jurisdiction.[6] The Tribunal ruled that only after the War began were these acts held to be have been committed in execution of war and were therefore crimes against humanity. Hence even though before World War II had begun one million Jews had been killed,[7] the Nuremberg Tribunal took a restrictive approach, some would argue unjustifiably and found only a crime against humanity if there was also proof of war crimes. This is an approach open to criticism but if we are relying upon legal precedents, then it is a

---

4. The United States, USSR, Britain and France concluded the London Agreement of August 8 1945. The Charter is annexed to the Agreement, 59 Stat. 1544, EAS no 472.
5. Art 6(c) International Military Tribunal Charter defined crimes against humanity. Agreement for the Prosecution and Punishment of the Major War Criminals of the European Axis Powers and Charter of the International Military Tribunal August 8 1945 82 UNTS 279.
6. Opinions and Judgement at 84. 'to constitute crimes against humanity , the acts relied on before the outbreak of war must have been in execution of, or in connection with, any crime within the jurisdiction of the Tribunal'. This would appear to narrow the Charter which is not so limited as article 6 includes as crimes against humanity 'inhumane acts committed against any civilian population, before or during the war.' See also Schick, The Nuremberg Trial and the International Law of the Future, 41, *American Journal of International Law,* 1947, 770.
7. Gilbert, *The Holocaust*.

restriction which has to be acknowledged.

The Austrian reparations agreement is also of little jurisprudential value for supporting claims for reparations for slavery as it was personal to the survivor and not to descendants. The belated damages agreement by Austria was narrow in its ambit and was only for the survivors of concentration camps. Indeed if a survivor dies before the claim is settled, the claim dies with the survivor. Any claim with respect to African slavery would be a claim by the survivors and beyond the Austrian crimes against humanity precedent.

There is unlike Nuremberg no question of individuals being punished and this begs the question of why construct an argument for reparations for slavery based on Nuremberg.

Nuremberg must also be placed in its historical context.[8] The reparations paid by Germany, Austria and Japan were among the terms for peace imposed by the victors and the conditions for reparations were set out in treaty form. Likewise the United Nations Convention on the Prevention of and Punishment of the Crime of Genocide 1948 which also includes within its definition of genocide 'killing members of the group', 'causing serious bodily or mental harm to members of the group' and 'forcibly transferring children of the group to another group'[9] does not apply retrospectively across the centuries.

The new Statute of the International Criminal Court also includes enslavement and deportation as crimes against humanity but the Court's jurisdiction will not be retrospective.[10]

There have been a number of acknowledgements of gross violations of human rights in previous centuries and reparation payments made to indigenous peoples. The Waikatu Raupatu Claims Settlement Act 1995, for example, under which the New Zealand Government paid substantial compensation for seizure of Maori lands by British settlers arose because of the breach, arguably of an earlier 1840 treaty. The same is true of many other indigenous settlements.

It is assumed, wrongly, that at the time of the African slave trade there were no international laws of which the slave traders were in violation.

8. Zalaquett, 'Balancing Ethical Imperatives and Political Constraints: The Dilemma of New Democracies Confronting Past Human Rights Violations', 43, *Hastings Law Journal*, 1992.

9. Article 2(a)(b)(e).

10. Rome Statute of the International Criminal Court reprod. in 39 ILM 999. Art. 7 (c) and (d).

Rather than relying upon Nuremberg or the Genocide Convention alternative approaches need to be found. The new approach is to argue that there is sufficient precedent but it is found elsewhere. Based upon this, there is sufficient precedent for a new charter to be negotiated to provide a framework for reparations for slavery.

This approach bases itself on the underlying principle of international human rights; that it is dynamic and purposive in the direction of greater protection of human rights.

In order for international legal precision it is necessary to distinguish between slavery and the slave trade.

In the first Treaty of Paris signed on 30 May 1814 between France and the United Kingdom it was agreed to suppress the traffic in slaves although the nature of the cooperation was unspecified and the slave trade could continue for five years.[11] The condemnation was reiterated at the Congress of Vienna in 1815.[12] Between 1815 and 1880 over fifty bilateral treaties were concluded.[13] The General Act of the Berlin Conference 1885 declared that 'trading in slaves is forbidden in conformity with the principles of international law.[14] This implies that the slave trade was illegal prior to the conclusion of the Berlin Conference Act as it is declaratory of existing general principles of international law. This begs the question of when the slave trade was illegal under general international legal principles.[15] Is it sometime between 1814 and 1885 or it earlier?

Critically the slave trade was also regarded by the United States and Britain in 1823 as piracy. It is an approach which fits in one with an authoritative international legal definition of piracy *jure gentium*,

> according to international law, piracy consists in sailing the seas for private ends without authorisation from the government of any state with the objection of committing Depredations upon property or acts of violence against persons.[16]

It does not limit the definition to robbery on the high seas.

This definition would appear to cover a significant proportion of the slave

11. Thomas, *The Slave Trade*, 1997, 583.
12. Robertson and Merrills, *Human Rights in the World*, 1992, 14.
13. *Ibid.* at 14.
14. There were 15 signatory powers.
15. Thomas, *op cit.* at 617.
16. League of Nations Document C 196, M 70, 1927, v. at 116.

trade, for example piracy was clearly in breach of international law in the seventeenth century when Grotius wrote in *De Jure Belli ac Pacis* and considered the pirate to be beyond the protection of any state.[17] Piracy was also a crime under English law in 1536 with 'An Act for the punishment of pirates and robbers of the sea'.[18]

This approach may bear much fruit as the reconceptualisation of piracy means that at the time of the commission of the slave trade it was illegal.

An examination of comparative national jurisprudence on the slave trade is also helpful. In 1771 in England in Somerset's Case a slave, James Somerset, was held in irons on board a ship on the Thames bound for Jamaica. Counsel's clarion plea that 'the air of England is too pure for any slave to breathe', was upheld by Lord Mansfield, so implying that slave trading was illegal and could not be enforced by English courts.[19]

Indeed the slave trade was regarded as 'worthy of condemnation and international response'[20] that it justified a violation of one of the fundamental principles of international law; freedom of the high seas.

The United Kingdom first abolished the slave trade and then later slavery in the colonies in 1832. Earlier in the eighteenth century slavery itself was abolished in France by the French revolution.[21]

There are also precedents of national reparations where no violation of national law had been found at the time. In the United States the Civil Liberties Act 1988 sought to make restitution to Japanese Americans for losses due to relocation and internment of US citizens and permanent resident aliens of Japanese ancestry during World War II. The Act also includes in its purposes to 'Apologise on behalf of the people of the United States.'[22] Yet the Supreme Court in *Korematsu* v. *United States* ruled at the time, that such internment was constitutional.[23]

This form of comparative historical jurisprudence is necessary if reliance is to be placed on a legal precedent approach.

---

17. Vol 2, cap 20, at 40. Grotius lived between 1583-1645.
18. Henry VIII. Cap 15.
19. See further, Van Bueren, 'Alleviating Poverty through the Constitutional Court', *South African Journal of Human Rights*, 1999, 52.
20. Randall, 'Universal Jurisdiction under International Law', 66 *Tex.L.Rev.* 785 at 794.
21. Although Napoleon tried to resurrect it.
22. Purpose (2).
23. 323 US 214 (1944).

But there is a second approach which can succeed even against those who assert that the problem with the African slave trade was that most of it was not in breach of international law or domestic law. This second approach overcomes the principal legal objection to a claim against reparations for the slavery and the slave trade of retrospectivity.

An international legal system is still one based largely upon state consent, and states are legally able to agree amongst themselves, even in the absence of any judicial action, to the principle of reparations for slavery and to evolve a mechanism for restitution.

There is nothing to prevent states deciding amongst themselves on how to consider the issue of reparations or to appoint a body to decide to whom, by whom, for what as well as the issue of the form of reparations and quantum.

The worrying point for some states would be that in departing from such fundamental principles of international law, it leaves them more vulnerable to claims for other historical human rights violations including colonialism. However, this vulnerability is significantly diminished if the slave trade were acknowledged as a form of piracy. The alternative is a lack of acknowledgement for wrongdoings which risks social amnesia.

To Whom, by Whom and for What?

The first question is who is eligible for reparations for slavery. If we accept that reparations can be paid for violations which occurred in previous centuries but whose effects can still be felt today, then we have to question why reparations should be limited to Africa and the descendants of Africans. What for example distinguishes African slavery from the slavery in the Caribbean and in South America.[24] Vattel even justified such slavery, arguing that if it was to convert Indians to Catholicism then such treatment was in accordance with international law.

It is at least arguable that for the some of the populations in South America and the Caribbean the effects of slavery are still felt today. This is not to argue that all descendants from all forms of slavery through time are entitled to reparations but the justifications for the boundaries have to be rigorously consistent for justice to be done.

---

24. Indeed Thomas's book, *The Slave Trade* is subtitled *The History of the Atlantic Slave Trade 1440-1870*.

The claim for reparations for the African slave trade are based on the destruction of civilisations, depopulation and the under-development of African states. Millions were forcibly removed and 'a patter of poverty and underdevelopment directly resulted'.[25] It was a crime against humanity for economic reasons. Reparations would be an economic reinstitution for an economic crime. Much of the wealth of the United Kingdom, for example was created from slavery.[26]

The claim for reparation has also been strenuously resisted. In a debate in the English House of Lords Lord Chesham resisted attempts that Britain should pay reparations by arguing that Benin and Niger Delta, where much of the slavery occurred are now 'amongst the densely populated parts of Africa.'[27] He also cited General Obasanjo, as he then was in 1991, on African impoverishment who argued that 'the major responsibility of our present impasse must be placed squarely on the shoulders of our leaders.'[28] However this argument can also be turned around. Without excusing corruption and crimes by present and past African leaders, slavery not only robbed those enslaved of their freedom but impoverished the societies from which they were taken. Reparations for slavery parallel actions against corrupt leaders for recovery of stolen funds.

There are also those who regard reparations as unacceptable on principle. This also happened in Israel where Menachim Begin held street demonstrations denouncing the Israeli government accepting German 'blood money'. Prime Minister David Ben Gurion asked Israel to accept German reparations reluctantly and for weighty reasons ie to obey the 'final injunction of the inarticulate six million, whose very murder was a ringing cry for Israel to rise, to be strong and prosperous, to safeguard her peace and security, and so prevent such a disaster from ever again overwhelming the Jewish people.'[29]

Just as complex is the question who ought to pay reparations. Historical evidence clearly shows the states which fostered and supported the slave trade. However, the liability extends beyond states to commercial entities and to par-

---

25. Gifford, 'The Legal Basis of the Claim for Reparations, Paper presented to the First Pan-African Congress on Reparations', Abuja, 1993. This is the first study of the legality of the reparations claim.
26. Viscount of Falkland in House of Lords debate on slavery and reparations, Hansard, 14 March 1996.
27. Lord Chesham resisting calls for British slavery reparations in House of Lords, *op cit*.
28. African Leadership Forum Conference, Nigeria cited in Hansard, *op cit*.
29. Schoenfield, Holocaust Reparations—A Growing Scandal, Commentary, September 2000.

ticular families. In the United States there have been apologies from companies which benefitted financially from slavery. In March 2000 Aetna Insurance apologised as have several newspapers which accepted advertisements from slave traders.[30] In California the Slaveholder Insurance Policy Law required all insurers whose businesses date to the 19th century to review their archives and reveal the names of insured slaves and their slaveholders.[31]

International reparations have also extended beyond the state. German companies agreed to pay £ 1.67 billion to those who were able to survive Nazi slave labour atrocities.[32]

There is also the question of slavery by Africans. In Ghana and in Benin chiefs have participated in ceremonies which offer apologies for the ancestors complicity in slavery.[33] The Ivory Coast film director, Gnoan M'bala, the director of Adanggamanican, an African film which looked at African involvement in the slave trade observes that, 'In our oral tradition slavery is left out purposefully because Africans are ashamed when we confront slavery. Let's wake up and look at ourselves through our own image.[34] If part of the purpose of reparations is for all of us to face the past and to educate ourselves, then reparations will be serving a similar role to that described by the Ministry of Culture and Art in Burkina Faso Da Bourdia about Adanggamanican, 'We need this kind of film to show our children this part of our history, that it happened among us in our own society.'

What Form of Compensation?

The principle behind the purpose of reparations was originally laid down by the Permanent Court of International Justice and is still valid today,[35]

30. In the United States at least ten cities including Chicago, Detroit and Washington have passed resolutions urging federal hearings into the impact of slavery. In January 2001 a Californian law required insurance companies to disclose policies they held covering losses incurred by slave owners when slaves died. *The Times*, January 2, 2001.

31. Passed in October 2000.

32. As of March 2001.

33. The Case for Slavery Reparations, Williams at http://news.mpr.org/features 20011/13.

34. Cited at Ivorian Film Focuses on African Hands in Slavery, Ouadraego, Associated Press www.nandotimes.com 2001. According to the director it was a film of 'fiction' with 'historical facts'.

35. The predecessor of the International Court of Justice at the Hague.

> 'reparation must, as far as possible, wipe out all the consequences of the illegal act and re-establish the situation which would, in all probability, have existed if that act had not been committed.'[36]

Reparations avoids a court judgement although it is a formal acknowledgement of a historical wrong and its continuing injury. It is symbolic of a commitment to redress with the participation of the victims or their descendants for guidance as to the nature and the quantum. A sum too small would be an insult and a sum too large would be unpayable.

Reparations for slavery are an opportunity for a flexible dynamic approach. There is likely to be very little reliance on individual claims. Indeed the nature of the reparations claim for slavery is the opposite of the individual claim. It is to restore dignity to groups and to acknowledge a mass wrongdoing and illegality.

The awards could be divided into two. Those directed towards states as debt relief payments paid directly to the state and those payments aimed at civil society groups focusing on social entitlements such as education and health. Reparations also address the barriers to enjoyment of human rights promoting the survival and participation of groups who were once at risk of perishing. In this sense reparations are transformative.

The discussions surrounding debt relief would take on a completely different hue. Reparations for slavery is also an opportunity to create a tool to address ongoing issues of inequality between developing and industrialised states. This does raise the question of whether the compensation culture is being used to replace a more equitable international order but it is not a question of either/or. In the past the linking of debt relief to poverty reduction has erroneously often been perceived as special pleading by African states. Arguably some of the debts owe their origin to remedying an impoverishment to which slavery may have contributed. Such an approach is supported by international human rights law. In a case against Surinam under the Inter-American Convention on Human Rights, the Aloeboetoe case, which is particularly apposite because of the difficulty in identifying the victim's descendants, the Court ordered the creation of trust funds and the reopening and staffing of a school.[37] Hence compensation does not have to be considered within a

36. Factory at Chorzow Jurisdiction , Judgement No 8 1927, PCIJ Series A No 9, 21. Factory at Chorzow Merits, Judgement No 13, 1928, PCIJ Series A No 17, 29.

37. Aloebeotoe et al, Reparations, Judgement of Inter-American Court of Human Rights, September 10, 1993.

narrow context. The carefully targeted cancellation of this debt is therefore not an issue only of relief but becomes a facet of compensation and therefore of justice.

The Need for an International Charter for Reparations of Slavery

Individual states could make reparations on an individual basis for slavery following the examples of the United States and Japanese Americans and Germany and Holocaust victims but this would not be as equitable as an international settlement. If payments were on a national basis than the descendants of slaves in Brazil, for example, may receive nothing whereas descendants of slaves in America may receive compensation. This is not to argue against groups in individual countries taking action but rather to argue for an internationally coordinated approach.

To have a consistent international approach there would need to be some form of international body or commission appointed to investigate the claim for reparations, to assess the quantum and to decide the form.

There has already been a claim for quantum. One body, the African World Reparations and Repatriation Truth Commission has set the figure at $777 trillion from former colonial states for slavery.[38] At first sight this may appear a grossly inflated sum but Germany has paid some 4 million claims, and a total of $55 billion has been disbursed both to the state of Israel and to individual victims.[39] Germany's gross violation of human rights continued for less than 25 years, while slavery was over a period of three centuries.

All of these issues are complex, but that is not a reason to shy away from them. Human rights has always been concerned with complex decisions. It is a reason for an international commission to be established to investigate the nature of the claim for reparations, the claimants and the nature of the payment. For such a commission to have international authority it needs to be set up under an international mandate such as an international charter. It would enjoy greater authority if the commission were set up under the auspices of

38. Meeting in Accra, August 1999.

39. Schoenfield, 'Holocaust Reparations—A Growing Scandal', Commentary, September 2000.

the United Nations. The United Nations Charter allows for this possibility.

The representation on the Commission needs not only to be global but also balanced as to gender.

If states, despite their responsibility for the slave trade and therefore piracy refuse to agree to the establishment of a commission there still remains the possibility of a Slavery Reparations Commission established by civil society. This would be following the precedent of the Women's International War Crimes Tribunal 2000 on Japanese Military Sexual Slavery.[40] The authority would come not from a state but from the global community to whom beneficiaries of the slave trade have a duty under international law to render account. As with the Women's International War Crimes Tribunal, a Slavery Reparations Commission would step into the vacuum left by the states rather than replacing their role. It would also help bring the former slave trading states to recognise their legal responsibility to provide reparations.

The Charter would not be the end of the process. The importance of the Slavery Reparations Commission is not only in its final result but also as with the South African Truth and Reconciliation Commission an educative and conscience-raising process both for the descendants of slaves and the descendants of the beneficiaries of slavery. Reparations for slavery are an opportunity for global society to reaffirm human values and to commit to the repetition in any form of the trafficking of men, women and children. It is an inescapable conclusion that had the international community responded earlier to calls for reparations, the continued trafficking in human beings would have been less likely.

---

40. See the summary judgement on http //home.atte.ne.jp/star/tribunal. The judges were Mcdonald, Argibay, Chinkin and Mutunga.

Judaism as a Source of Human Rights

Asher Maoz*

A. Judaism

Judaism—*Yahadut* in Hebrew—is first and foremost a religion. The term Judaism—*Judaismes* in the Greek form—is first found in the Jewish-Helenistic literature of the first century as a synonym for 'the religion of the Israelites'.[1] The same sense is found in St Paul's Epistles to the Galatians—'And profited in the Jews' religion'.[2]

This term does not appear in the Bible[3] or in rabbinical literature and only occasionally is found in medieval literature. In classical sources the term used

---

* Associate Professor of Law, Tel Aviv University. General editor of Law, Society and Culture—The Buchman Faculty of Law Series.

1. *Maccabees* II, 2:21; 8:1; 14:38.

2. 1:14, King James Version. Other versions translate this term as 'Judaism', *see e.g.* E.J. Goodspeed, *The Parallel New Testament: The American Translation and the King James Version* (Chicago & London, 1943) 432.

3. Save for the verb *mityahadim*, [becoming Jewish] in *Esther* 8:17. The term *yehudim* originally meant 'the inhabitants of the kingdom of Yehuda', later it gained the meaning 'Jews'.

Raphael Walden (ed.), Racism and Human Rights, *55-83.*

for the body of Jewish teachings is *Torah*. The term Judaism became popular during the Age of Enlightenment.[4] Judaism, as an appellation, means Jewish Religion[5] and as such is equivalent to Christianity or other named religions. However, this is only partially true, for Judaism is also a comprehensive legal system. In their famous work *Major Legal Systems in the World Today—An Introduction to the Comparative Study of Law*,[6] R. David & J. Brierly define Judaism as 'essentially a religion of the law.'[7] '[T]he Catholic Church', on the other hand, '...did...feel it unnecessary to develop a Christian law to take the place of Roman law... Canon law was not a complete legal system designed to replace Roman law. It complemented Roman law or other "private" laws, never anything more, and regulated subjects not covered by these laws such as Church organization, the sacraments, and canonical procedure.'[8] The separation between spiritual and temporal matters, which is at the foundation of Christianity,[9] is alien to Judaism for Judaism encompasses all aspects of society and of an individual's life.[10] As Professor Freiman wrote:

> Jewish religion and law are a single entity. The *Torah* makes no dogmatic distinction between religious teachings and legal provisions.[11]

In addition, Judaism is an ethical system, teaching a moral way of life: 'Jewish law is a combined system, consisting of law, religion and morality. These three

4. *Encyclopaedia Judaica*, 16 vols. (1971-72), X, 383; *Encyclopaedia Hebraica*, 32 vols., (1968) XIX, 159 (*Heb.*).

5. *The Oxford Dictionary of the Jewish Religion* (New York & Oxford: R.J. Werblowsky & G. Wigoder eds., 1997), in the entry "Judaism" refer to "Jewish Religion"; at p. 382; *Encyclopaedia Britannica* defines Judaism as "the religion of the Jews": *Macropaedia*, vol. 10, p. 623; *Micropaedia*, vol. 5, p. 244. The 1971 edition of *Encyclopaedia Britannica* defined Judaism as "the Hebrew religion"; vol. 13, p. 103.

6. R. David & J. Brierly, *Major Legal Systems in the World Today—An Introduction to the Comparative Study of Law* (London, 1985).

7. *Ibid.*, at 456.

8. *Ibid.*, at 464.

9. This distinction was expressed in Matthew's rule: *"Reddite ergo quae sunt Caesaris, Caesari; et quae sunt Dei Deo"*; *Matthew*, XXII, 21. *See, generally*, A. Maoz, 'The Rabbinate and the Rabbinical Courts Between the Hammer and the Anvil', 16-17 (1990-1991) *Shenaton Hamishpat Ha'Ivri* [Jewish Law Annual], 289, 311-312 (*Heb.*).

10. A. Maoz, 'State and Religion In Israel', in *International Perspectives on Church and State* (M. Mor (ed.), Omaha, 1993), 239, 242.

11. A.H. Freiman, 'Jewish Law in the Land of Israel', 5704 [1944] *Ha'aretz Calendar*, 110 (*Heb.*).

elements are intertwined and interrelated, and form one system, known as *Halacha*, which means a way of life.'[12]

B. Judaism and Human Rights

The fact that Judaism is not merely a religious system dealing solely with the relations between man and God may account for the fact that even non-religious people accept its teachings and norms. However, further explanation is needed for the thesis that Judaism has and continues to serve as a valuable source of human rights. The explanation is found in the fact that the civil and ethical tenets of Judaism, not less than its 'religious' aspects, stem from divinity. The Ten Commandments include religious norms, such as the forbidding of idolatry; ethical principles, such as the commandment to respect one's parents; social values, exemplified by the universal day of rest; moral rules as in the prohibition of adultery and legal provisions, such as the prohibition against false testimony. All these norms were given by God on Mount Sinai and are equally binding. From a religious point of view there is no distinction between the religious and civil norms of *Halacha*.[13]

12. Ch. Povarsky, in 'The Enforcement of a Jewish Marriage Contract in a Civil Court: Is Jewish Law a Religious Law?', (April 2000) *Jewish Law Report*, 1, 3.

13. The interplay between religious and legal norms in *Halacha* may be demonstrated through the controversy as to whether paying a debt is a legal duty or merely a religious one. This controversy is reported in the *Babylonian Talmud* [a collection of commentaries and expositions on the *Mishna*—a codification of post-Biblical oral law, circa year 200—compiled in Babylon in the sixth century. Reference to the *Talmud*, or to a tractate in general, is always to the *Babylonian Talmud*], Tractate *Ketuboth* 86a. One of the Sages expressed the view that a debtor is under a legal obligation to pay his debt, just as a bailee is under an obligation to return the bailed chattel to the bailor. Another Sage rejected this comparison, stating that the bailor's right to demand the return of the bailed chattel is based on the fact that he retains the title to the chattel. In contrast, a loan is usually spent and does not remain in the hands of the debtor. Therefore, the obligation to pay the debt rests on the debtor's promise. The obligation to fulfill this promise is based on a religious commandment, as 'paying off a debt is a *mitzva*' [a religious commandment]. When asked what is the rule if the debtor abstains from fulfilling this obligation, the Sage answered that just as a Rabbinical Court may enforce religious obligations, so too the Court will compel performance of the religious obligation to pay a debt. *See, generally*, M. Elon, *Jewish Law—History, Sources, Principles*, 4 vols. (B. Auerbach & M. Sykes, (trans.), Philadelphia and Jerusalem, 1994), I, 117-9.

It might seem surprising that Jewish law, being a religious legal system, incorporates principles of human rights. *Prima facie*, such values and principles contradict a religious normative system in which the ultimate task of the individual is to serve God.[14] This is especially so since Judaism does not propound a concept of rights but adheres to a concept of duties, not only in the relationship between man and God, but also in the relationship between man and man. Indeed, even the term 'human rights' is absent in Jewish classic texts,[15] as is the term 'rights' in general. Yet while 'Jewish law... postulates a system of duties rather than a system of rights',[16] the protection of these rights might actually be more effective under such a system.[17] Evidence of this may be found in relation to the right to life. This right is paramount in Western civilization, nonetheless, an American court stated a century ago that failing to rescue a two-year old baby seen on a railroad track would not comprise a breach of the law. The by-stander 'may be styled a ruthless savage and a moral monster', the learned judge tells us, 'but he is not liable in damages for the child's injury, or indictable under the statute for his death'.[18]

No 'right to life' exists in Jewish law, yet the *Torah* commands us: 'Neither shalt thou stand against the blood of thy neighbour'.[19] This duty takes precedence over almost every other commandment. Maimonides summarized this rule as follows:

> If one is able to save another and does not save him, he transgresses the... injunction, *neither shalt thou stand idly by the blood of thy neighbour*.[20]

---

14. Y. Leibovitch, *Judaism, Human Values and the Jewish State* (Cambridge, Mass., 1992), 14.
15. M.R. Konvitz, 'Introduction', in M.R. Konvitz (ed.), *Judaism and Human Rights* (New York, 1972), 13.
16. H.H. Cohn, *Human Rights in Jewish Law* (New York, 1984), 18. *Cf.* A. Kirschenbaum, *Equity in Jewish Law—Beyond Equity: Halakhic Aspirationism in Jewish Civil Law* (Hoboken, New Jersey, 1991), 1-8.
17. *Cf.* R.M. Cover, 'Obligations: A Jewish Jurisprudence of the Social Order', (1987) 5 *J. L. & Religion* 65. Rene Cassin, who was assigned to write the first draft of the Universal Declaration of Human Rights, expressly mentioned the duties of man. This idea met with objections from members of the United Nations Commission on Human Rights, both on liberal and religious grounds; R. Cassin, 'From the Ten Commandments to the Rights of Man', in *Of Law and Man—Essays in Honor of Haim H. Cohn* (S. Shoham, (ed.), New York and Tel-Aviv, 1971), 13, 14.
18. *Buch v. Amory Manufacturing Co.* 44 A. 809, 810 (1898).
19. *Leviticus* 19:16.
20. Maimonides, *Torts*, 'Murder and Preservation of Life', 1:14.

Failure to save human life is tantamount to actively shedding blood.[21]

C. Human Dignity

A major crossroad where Western philosophy intersects with Judaism is human dignity. Human dignity is at the core of central international instruments including the Charter of the United Nations, 1945, the Universal Declaration of Human Rights, 1948, and the Human Rights Covenant, 1966. These documents regard human rights as deriving from the 'inherent dignity' of the human being.[22]

Several national constitutions, particularly those of recent origin as is the German *Grundgesetz*, explicitly recognize human dignity; however, constitutions which do not expressly refer to human dignity are not necessarily indifferent to it. An American writer even stated:

> The basic value in the United States Constitution, broadly conceived, has become a concern for human dignity.[23]

Another writer noted:

> Understood abstractly enough, the right to human dignity would gain unanimous adherence in the United States and in many if not all other contemporary societies.[24]

As with human rights, the term 'dignity' is absent from Jewish writings and in fact there is no parallel term in Hebrew. While the Hebrew term *kavod* literally means 'honour', Justice Cohn has taken the term *kevod ha-beriot* ('the honour of the creatures'), as used by the sages, and correctly translated it as human dignity.[25] This value which underlines the teachings of Judaism is supreme and even supersedes the commandments of God.[26]

---

21. Tractate *Sanhedrin* 4:5. *See, generally,* A. Kirschenbaum, 'The "Good Samaritan" and Jewish Law', (1976) 7 *Dine Israel* [an annual of Jewish and Israeli family law] 7.
22. *See, generally,* H.H. Cohn, "On the Meaning of Human Dignity", (1983) 13 *Israel Yearbook on Human Rights* [*IYHR*] 226.
23. W.F. Murphy, 'An Ordering of Constitutional Values', (1980) 53 *Southern California Law Review* [*South. Cal. L. Rev.*] 703, 745.
24. P. Brest, 'Accommodation of the Majoritarianism and Rights of Human Dignity', (1980) 53 *South. Cal. L. Rev.* 761, 762.
25. H.H. Cohn, n. 21 above, 247.
26. *Babylonian Talmud,* Tractate *Berakhot* 19b.

Human dignity stems from creation itself. We are told in *Genesis*[27] that man was created in the very image of God. Thomas Paine regarded this Biblical source as proof 'that the equality of man, far from being a modern doctrine is the oldest on record' and relied on it to support the principle in the American Declaration of Independence that all men are created equal.[28]

This succinct Biblical statement may well be regarded as the basis of human rights in Judaism. The variety of interpretations accorded to this verse cover most aspects of human dignity and freedom. The full verse reads as follows:

> And God said: 'Let us make man in our image after our likeness'... So God created man in His own image, in the image of God created He him, male and female created He them.

The Psalmist described man as not worthy to be within the contemplation of God, yet he asserted:

> [T]hou hast made him a little lower than God,[29] and thou crownest him with glory and majesty.[30]

Ben Azzai, a fourth-century Jewish scholar, inferred from this verse that all descendants of Adam—regardless of religion, race or colour—bear the imprint of divine creation and divine likeness and must be treated accordingly.[31]

Here it is relevant to mention a traditional commentary explaining why God created a single man, Adam, as opposed to a community of men: 'Therefore each one ought to say: "It is for me alone that the world was created"'. This idea is given practical application in the caution administered by the Jewish Religious Courts to witnesses in criminal cases. The Court must warn the witnesses not to give hearsay or speculative evidence:

> Man was created single to teach that whoever destroys one human life is deemed by Scriptures to have destroyed the whole universe and if a man saves a single soul, Scriptures regards him as having saved the whole world.[32]

27. *Genesis* 1:26-27.
28. T. Paine, *The Rights of Man* (London, 1915), 43.
29. Interestingly, the King James translation could not accept the idea that man is just a little lower than God and replaced God with 'the angels'.
30. *Psalms* 8:6-7.
31. *Sifra* [a collection of interpretations of *Leviticus*, compiled in the fourth century], *Kedoshim* 4:12.
32. *Mishna*, Tractate *Sanhedrin* 4:5. *Cf.* the version in Maimonides, *Book of Judges*, 16b.

Another interesting reason given for the creation of a single individual is 'that no one may be heard to say to another: "My father was greater than yours"'.[33] This reminds us of another statement in the Bible: 'Have we not all one father? Hath not one God created us?'[34]

The statement has more than philosophical value as God commanded the Children of Israel:

> One law and one manner shall be for you and for the stranger that sojourneth with you.[35]

The idea of equality is expressed in the description of the covenant between God and the Children of Israel. Abba Hillel Silver wrote:

> Judaism was essentially a democratic faith, a people's religion. The covenant was made with 'all the men of Israel, from the hewer of your wood to the drawer of your water' (*Deuteronomy* 29:11). The *Torah* was given to all and in sight of all (*Exodus* 19). The entire people was summoned to become a 'kingdom of priests and a holy nation' (*Exodus* 19:6)... On the verse: 'You stand this day all of you before the Lord your God, your heads, your tribes, your elders, and your officers, all the men of Israel' (*Deuteronomy* 29:10), a *midrash* expounds: God says: 'Even though I have appointed over you heads and judges, elders and officers, you are all equal in my sight'. This is the meaning of 'all the men of Israel'—all are alike (*Midrash Tanhuma*).[36]

The rule of law and equality before the law are universally applied in Judaism. We find, in Jewish ancient sources, two versions of a story relating to the status of kings in judicial proceedings.

The *Babylonian Talmud* tells of Alexander Yannai, a powerful king, whose slave stood trial for killing a person. Rabbi Simeon Ben Shetah, President of the *Sanhedrin*, the ancient Jewish Court, summoned the king to be present at the trial. The king appeared in court yet rejected Rabbi Ben Shetah's demand to stand during the trial. Rabbi Ben Shetah's reprimanded the king, saying:

> Stand up on thy feet, King Yannai, and let the witnesses testify against thee; yet it is not before us that thou standest, but before Him who spoke and the world came into

33. *Ibid.*
34. *Malachi* 2:10.
35. *Numbers* 15:16. *See also, Exodus* 12:49.
36. A.H. Silver, *Where Judaism Differed* (New York, 1956), 275-6.

> being, as it is written [in the *Torah*], 'Then both the men between whom the controversy is, shall stand before the Lord' (*Deuteronomy* 19:17).[37]

Yet the king refused to stand up saying he would not obey Rabbi Ben Shetah, but would obey what the other members of the court would decide. Thereupon, the Talmud tells us, Ben Shetach turned his eyes on his colleagues, yet they all looked down at the ground out of fear of the king. Ben Shetach reacted with temper, saying: 'Are ye wrapped in thoughts? Let the Master of thoughts—meaning God—come and call you to account'. Thereupon 'Gabriel came and smote them to the ground, and they died'. Following this episode it was enacted: 'A King may neither judge nor been judged'.

It is clear why this traumatic occurence caused the sages to grant immunity to the kings. It is less obvious why they were enjoined from sitting as judges in trials. In order to understand the reason for that we must look up at the beginning of the section. It is stated there that this rule applies to the kings of Israel only, but not to the kings of the house of David. The sages learned this from the words of Jeremiah the prophet: 'O House of David, thus saith the Lord, execute judgment in the morning and and deliver him that is robbed out of the hand of the oppressor...'[38]. And how do we know that they may be judged? The Talmud explains: '... and if they may not be judged, how could they judge?'. This logic is in accordance with Resh Lakish's statement: 'Adorn yourself first and then adorn others'.

A different version of this story appears in *Midrash Tanhuma*, a homiletic interpretation of the Scripture, attributed to Rabbi Tanhum Bar Abba, of the second half of the fourth century. According to that source a plaintiff asked Ben Shetach to summon a Hasmonean king to a civil suit. Ben Shetach checked with his colleagues whether they would try the king without fear. Upon their positive answer he summoned the king, who refused to stand and answer the claim. The story about the angel who smote the members of the court to death has here an addendum: 'the king was shocked. Immediately Simeon Ben Shetah said to him: "Stand up on thy feet, and answer the claim, yet it is not before myself that thou standest, but before Him who spoke and the world came into being, as it is written: 'Then both the men between whom the controversy is, shall stand before the Lord'. Instantly he rose to his feet and was sued"'.[39]

---

37. Tractate *Sanhedrin* 19. The translation is from the Soncino edition, by J. Shechter (I. Epstein, ed.). However, the transliteration of the names is that of *Encyclopaedia Judaica*.

38. Jer. 21:12.

39. *Midrash Tanhuma*, Judges, 7.

This episode was cited by the *Midrash* as a demonstration of the Biblical warning against discrimination in justice and against preferential treatment. This is expressed in the prohibition of having the poor litigant stand while the rich counterpart remains sitting. The *Midrash* concludes: 'The judges must regard it as if the Divine Presence were sitting among them, as it is written: "Amidst God will he judge'"[40]

God himself is subject to the rule of law. *The Jerusalem Talmud*[41] states:

> It is universal custom that when an earthly king issues a decree, at his will he observes it himself, and at his will only others are bound to observe it. But it is otherwise with the Holy One Blessed Be He, for He is Himself the first to observe all his decrees. This

---

40. Psalms, 82:1. A third version of this story appears in Flavius Josephus' book *Jewish Antiquities*. According to Josephus, the episode told in the Talmud related to Herod, the ruler of the Galilee, who was summond by king Hyrcanus to court to stand trial for committing murder. Yet, Sextus, the governor of Syria, threatened the king to acquit Herod of the charge. The governor's letter indeed 'gave Hyrcanus a pretext for letting Herod go without suffering any harm from the Synhedrion [*Sanhedrin*]'. Josephus reports that Herod appeared before the *Sanhedrin* escorted by his troops, and frightened both the witnesses and judges. Samaias, a member of the *Sanhedrin* arose and said: 'Fellow councillors and King, I do not myself know of, nor do I suppose that you can name, anyone who when summoned before you for trial has ever presented such an appearance. For no matter who it was that came before this Synhedrion for trial, he has shown himself humble and has assumed the manner of one who is fearful and seeks mercy from you... But this fine fellow Herod, who is accused of murder and has been summoned on no less grave a charge than this, stands here... with his soldiers round him, in order to kill us if we condemn him as the law prescribes, and to save himself by outraging justice. But it is not Herod whom I should blame for this or for putting his own interests above the law, but you and the king, for giving him such great licence . Be assured, however, that God is great , and this man, whom you now wish to release for Hyrcanus' sake, will one day punish you and the king as well'. Indeed, when Herod assumed royal power, he killed Hyrcanus and all members of the *Sanhedrin*, save for Samaias; Josephus, *Jewish Antiquities*, Book 14, Chap. 4 (Cambridge: R. Marcus, trans., 1943) vol. 7, p. 539-543. Interestingly, based on Josephus' account, Rabbi Adret Solomon Ben Abraham [the *RaShBa*], one of the foremost Jewish scholars in the twelfth century, in his interpretation to tractate *Sanhedrin*, regarded the account in the *Babylonian Talmud* erroneous, and suggested that the person charged before the *Sanhedrin* was Herod and not King Yannai. This is also the opinion of several researchers; see: Y. Ephron, 'Simeon Ben Shetah and King Yannai', In Memory of Gedaliahu Alon: *Essays in Jewish History and Philology* (Tel-Aviv: M. Dorman, S. Safrai & M. Stern eds., 1970) 69, 94-98 (*Heb.*)

41. Known also as the *Palestinian Talmud*, concluded in the second half of the fourth century.

is deduced from the text 'And ye shall observe that which I observe... I am the Lord' (*Leviticus* 22:9). That is to say, I, the Lord am the first to observe the commandments of the *Torah*.[42]

A vivid demonstration of the idea of the *Torah*'s supremacy over its Giver is to be found in the *Babylonian Talmud*. The *Talmud* tells us of a *Halachic* dispute that arose between the *Tannaim* (Sages who lived in the first two centuries), in which, notwithstanding that all the Sages disagreed with Rabbi Eliezer, the latter tried to convince his colleagues that justice lay with him. We are told:

On that day Rabbi Eliezer brought forward every imaginable argument, but they [the Sages] did not accept them. Said he to them: 'If the *Halacha* [Law] agrees with me, let this carob tree prove it! Thereupon the carob tree was torn a hundred cubits out of its place—others affirm, four hundred cubits'. 'No proof can be brought from a carob tree', they retorted. Again he said to them: 'If the *Halacha* agrees with me, let the stream of water prove it!' Whereupon the stream of water flowed backwards. 'No proof can be brought from a stream of water', they rejoined. Again he urged: 'If the *Halacha* agrees with me, let the walls of the schoolhouse prove it', whereupon the walls began to lean. But Rabbi Joshua rebuked them, saying: 'When scholars are engaged in a *Halachic* dispute, what have ye to interfere?' Hence they did not fall, in honour of Rabbi Joshua, nor did they resume the upright position, in honour of Rabbi Eliezer; and they are still standing thus inclined. Again said he to them: 'If the *Halacha* agrees with me, let it be proven from heaven!' Whereupon a Heavenly Voice cried out, 'Why do ye dispute with Rabbi Eliezer, seeing that in all matters the *Halacha* agrees with him!' But Rabbi Joshua arose and exclaimed, 'It is not in heaven' (*Deuteronomy* 30:12). What did he mean by this? Said Rabbi Jeremiah: 'The *Torah* has already been given at Mount Sinai; we pay no attention to a Heavenly Voice, because Thou hast long since written in the Torah at Mount Sinai, "After the majority must one incline"' (*Exodus* 23:2).[43]

There is an addendum to this legend:

Rabbi Nathan met Elijah [the prophet] and asked him: 'What did the Holy One, Blessed Be He, do in that hour?'—'He laughed [with joy]', he replied. saying: 'My sons have defeated Me, my sons have defeated Me!'.[44]

42. Tractate *Rosh Hashana*, Chap. 1, p. 57a.

43. Tractate *Baba Mezia* 59b.

44. *Ibid*.

Commenting on these two *Talmudic* passages, the late Justice Moshe Silberg of the Supreme Court of Israel, wrote:

> Here we find the Rule of Law in the absolute sense of the term: The law ruling the lawgiver; the inclusion of the legislator himself within the framework of legal and decisional relationships created by the laws given by him. He observes 'the precepts of the Law', submits to the authority of the law, and furthermore submits to the authentic interpretation given by the interpreters, *i.e.*, submits himself to the jurisdiction of an authoritative body, the majority, authorized by him to determine in case of doubt, which for him is of course no doubt at all. If the law is 'After the majority must one follow', then this rule is to be applied even when the lawgiver himself is an interested party.[45]

Justice Silberg summarizes:

> The idea is too great to be grasped by our ordinary mind, but one conclusion certainly rises from it: that the jurisdiction of Jewish law is not confined within the boundaries of relations between man and man. Matters concerning the relationship between man and God... are caught by the net of legal relations as well.[46]

Of special interest is the role of justice in Judaism. George Foot Moore stated:

> In no sphere is the influence of the highest conceptions of Judaism more manifestly determinative than in that to which we give the general name of justice, including under it, *first*, fair dealing between man and man, the distributive justice which gives to each his due; *second*, public justice, the function of the community in defining and enforcing the duties and rights of individuals and classes; and, *third*, rectitude, or integrity of personal character. In all parts of the Bible, justice in the broad sense is the fundamental virtue on which human society is based. It is not less fundamental in the idea of God, and in the definition of what God requires of man.[47]

---

45. M. Silberg, 'Law and Morals in Jewish Jurisprudence', (1961)75 *Harvard Law Review* [*Harv. L. Rev.*] 306, 310-11. A revised version of the article is included as chapter 6 in M. Silberg, *Talmudic Law and the Modern State* (New York: B-Z Bosker, trans., 1973). See, however, I. Englard, 'Majority Decision vs. Individual Truth: The Interpretation of the "Oven of Achnai" Aggadah', 15: 1-2 *Tradition* 137.

46. *Ibid.*

47. G.F. Moore, *Judaism in the First Centuries of the Christian Era: The Age of the Tannaim*, 3 vols., (Cambridge Ma., 1927) I, 180.

E. Judaism, Human Rights and Western Philosophy

Western notions of human rights and democratic values have derived much of their substance from the Old Testament as well as from classic Judaic sources. Thus, Lecky wrote in his famous work *History of the Rise and Influence of the Spirit of Rationalism in Europe*:[48]

> It is a historical fact that in the large majority of cases, the Protestant advocates of civil rights took most of their principles from the Old Testament, whereas the advocates of oppression took most of their principles from the New Testament.

The American Bill of Rights is based to a large extent on the constitutions of the colonies which themselves drew extensively from the Old Testament.[49] The Puritan settlers of the first colonies of Plymouth and Massachusetts Bay chose the ancient laws of the Hebrews as their governing legal system. An American jurist colourfully depicted Jewish law sailing to America 'aboard the Mayflower and the Alberta' and striking 'deep roots in rocky New England.'[50] A writer of that period asserted that 'the people of Massachusetts adopted the laws of Moses.'[51] Moreover, it has been stated that '[t]he legacy of Hebrew laws... was to remain part of the American heritage.'[52] A contemporary American jurist states:

> The fundamental liberties of man—as they are stated in the Bill of Rights or in the Universal Declaration of Human Rights—find their roots in the narratives and prophets of the Hebrew Scriptures and the teachings they have generated over the centuries.[53]

Another American jurist went so far as to declare that '[t]he Hebrew Bible [serves] as the primary source of American civilization.'[54]

---

48. Vol. II, 168 (rev. ed., 1871).

49. On Puritan constitutionalism as 'a fertile seed-bed out of which American constitutionalism grew', *see* J. Witte, 'How to Govern a City On a Hill: The Early Puritan Contribution to American Constitutionalism', (1990) 39 *Emory Law Journal* 41, 62.

50. B. J. Meislin, *Jewish Law in American Tribunals* (New York, 1976), IX.

51. H. St. G. Tucker, *Commentaries on the Laws of Virginia* 1, 6-7 (Winchester, 1831).

52. Meislin, *Jewish Law*, n. 50 above, 28.

53. Konvitz, *Judaism*, n. 15 above, 17.

54. J.S. Auerbach, *Rabbis and Lawyers: The Journey From Torah to the Constitution* (Bloomington IN, 1990), xvii.

Mr. Justice Brandeis was equally bold in his attribution, stating that 'twentieth century ideals of America had been the age-old ideas of the Jew.'[55]

Professor Suzanne Stone has criticized the heavy reliance placed on Jewish law in American legal thinking. She writes:

> ... the Jewish legal tradition has come to represent in this scholarship precisely the model of law that many contemporary American theorists propose for American legal society.[56]

Extensive references to Biblical law as well as to classic Jewish sources are found in American judicial decisions.[57] In an article dealing with 'Maimonides and American Case Law'[58] Bernard Meislin noted that 'a computerized search of recent American legal decisions retrieves citations of Maimonides as authority for American legal propositions in the fields of criminal law, matrimonial law, bailment, arbitration, real estate, evidence and even corporate litigation'. He concludes: 'Despite divergent legal systems, despite a sea change in culture and a different language, *Halacha* as ordered by Maimonides, speaks to American judges of the late twentieth century with a persuasive voice... .'[59]

The first settlers in America brought the seeds of Biblical law from their English homeland. Jewish law had played a major role in the old world. Jewish rabbinical sources were cited in English courts and consulted by the English legislature as early as in the sixteenth century.[60] The theoretical basis for the application of Biblical law was supplied by a book from the sixteenth century,

55. A. Gal, *Brandeis of Boston* (Cambridge, Mass., 1980), 126.

56. S.L. Stone, 'In Pursuit of the Counter-Text: The Turn to the Jewish Legal Model in Contemporary American Legal Theory', 106 *Harv. L. Rev.* 813, 819 (1993).

57. *See* D. A. Ashburn, 'Appealing to a Higher Authority? Jewish Law in American Judicial Opinions', (1994) 71 *Univ. of Detroit Mercy L. Rev.* 295. *See also*, B. Meislin, 'Jewish Law in America', in *Jewish Law in Legal History and the Modern World* (B.S. Jackson (ed.), Leiden, 1980); *Idem*, 'The Ten Commandments in American Law', in *Jewish Law and Current Legal Problems* (N. Rakover (ed.), Jerusalem, 1984), 109.

58. In *Maimonides as Codifier of Jewish Law* (N. Rakover (ed.), Jerusalem, 1987), 269.

59. *Ibid.*, at 270.

60. See 'Proceedings Against James Naylar and Charles II' in Corbett's *Collection of State Trials* (1565); cf. Abrahams I. & Sayle C.E., 'The Purchase of Hebrew Books by the English Parliament in 1647', (1918) *Jewish Historical Society of England: Transactions*, 63. This occurred notwithstanding the fact that the Jews had been expelled from England under a Royal order (*Statutum de Judaismo*) issued by King Edward I in 1275 and only repealed in 1656.

Examen Legum Angliae: Or the Laws of England Examined by Scripture, Antiquity and Reason.[61] In this book the author distinguishes between two sets of laws in the Bible: laws which deal with religious worship and laws which relate to the Kingdom of Israel. The former are designated for Jews only. The latter consisting of judgments which are 'Laws of Common Justice and Equity belonging to the moral law', have been given to the Jews as human beings and also apply to non-Jews, and as such were also to be applied in England. The author refers to a successful experiment conducted by King Alfred at the end of the ninth century, to enforce the laws of Moses throughout his kingdom. The king regarded the judgments specified in chapters 20-23 of *Exodus* 'the most apt and compatible for the government of his kingdom'.

The reliance on Biblical and other Judaic sources is not unique to American scholars. While stating that '[t]he spirit prevailing during the preparation of the Universal Declaration of Human Rights was completely at variance with any intention of drawing deliberate and direct inspiration from the Ten Commandments', and while 'any relationship between the Universal Declaration... and the Decalogue as the first formulation of man's basic duties... is not a formal one', yet it 'does exist' and 'its reality is evident',[62] for 'the Decalogue... is the point of departure, and the present Charter ... is our temporary point of arrival'.[63]

F. Contemporary Application of Jewish Values

In 1979 criminal proceedings were instituted in Israel against a Jewish husband who had forced himself on his wife.[64] In his defence against the charge of rape, the husband relied upon the well established common law rule that by virtue of

61. Published in 1656, attributed to A. Boots. Excerpts from the book were published in M. De Wolfe, *Readings in American Legal History* (Cambridge, 1949).

62. Cassin, n. 16 above, 14.

63. *Ibid.*, at 22. When asked about the sources from which he derived the principles of the Universal Declaration of Human Rights, Rene Cassin is said to have answered that he had just rephrased the Ten Commandments; A. Rubinstein, *Constitutional Law of the State of Israel*, 2 vols. (5th ed., Jerusalem & Tel-Aviv, 1996), 907 (*Heb.*). Rubinstein makes no reference to any specific source for this anecdote; it is certainly not supported by Cassin's article.

64. Cr. F. [Criminal File] 163/79, *State of Israel v. Cohen*, 5740(1) P.M [*Psakim Mehozi'im* = Law Reports of the District Courts] 245.

a marriage contract a wife is under a duty to cohabit, an essential component of which is to consent to sexual relations. A husband cannot, therefore, be convicted of raping his wife, as this offence is committed only if sexual intercourse takes place without the woman's consent.[65] The Court rejected the common law defence which is based on ecclesiastical law, as inapplicable to Jews in Israel.

This decision was upheld on appeal.[66] The Court based its decision on Jewish family law which applies to Jewish couples under Israeli law.[67] Under this law, although a wife is under a marital obligation to have intercourse with her husband, the common law doctrine of the husband's 'domain' over his wife and of the wife's 'submission' to him is totally unacceptable, and the husband is prohibited from forcing himself upon her. To use Maimonides' words: 'The wife is not a captive taken by sword to please her master's desires'.[68] Justice Bechor of the Supreme Court summarized the decision as follows:

> The conclusion... is consistent with the fundamental principles of protecting a woman as a free person, not as a slave subject to the whims of her husband on such a sensitive matter which, unfortunately, has not been embodied in the legislation or judicial opinions of some of the most enlightened and progressive nations... The Jewish people should be proud of the progressive and liberal approach of its traditions and Halacha on the subject throughout the ages.[69]

The common law rule, on the other hand, 'does not fit human dignity and the dignity of the marriage institute'.[70]

---

65. M. Hale, 1 *The History of the Pleas of the Crown* (1773) 629.

66. Cr. A. [Criminal Appeal] 91/80, *Cohen v. State of Israel*, 35(3) P.D [*Piskei Din* = Law Reports of the Supreme Court] 281.

67. Rabbinical Law Jurisdiction (Marriage and Divorce) Law, 1953, 7 *Laws of the State of Israel* (LSI) 139; A. Maoz, 'Enforcement of Religious Courts' Judgments Under Israeli Law', (1991) 33 *Journal of Church & State* 473, 473-75; A. Maoz, 'Religious Human Rights in the State of Israel', in *Religious Human Rights in Global Perspective—Legal Perspectives* (J.D. van der Vyver & J. Witte Jr. (ed.), 1996) 349, 354-57.

68. Maimonides, *Laws of Marriage* 14:9. Compare this language with Hume's harsh assertion that '[T]he husband... cannot... commit a rape on his own wife, who has surrendered her person to him in this regard', Hume, *The Commentaries on the Law of Scotland Respecting the Description and Punishment of Crimes*, (4th ed. by Bell, 1984) vol. 1, 306. See also N. Rakover, 'Coercion of Conjugal Relations', *Jewish Law and Current Legal Problems* (N. Rakover (ed.), Jerusalem, 1984) 137.

69. N. 66 above, at 291, *per* Bechor J.

70. Quoted from Justice Halevi's opinion in Cr. A. 353/62, *El Fakir v. A.G.*, 18(4) P.D. 200, 219.

The rationale underlying the *Cohen* decision is questionable. The common law rule became part of the Palestinian Criminal Code of 1936.[71] This Code became part of Israeli law when, upon its establishment, the State of Israel adopted Mandatory law.[72] Section 152 of the Code specifically provides that only 'unlawful' sexual intercourse with a woman, which takes place 'without her consent', constitutes rape, while under the common law, sexual intercourse with a wife is 'always lawful'.[73] Arguably, religious law, which applies in Israel in matters of marriage and divorce, should have no bearing on this issue. Moreover, concern has been expressed that the *Cohen* decision might discriminate against wives whose religious law permits their husbands to have sexual intercourse without their consent.[74] Yet, when a further case involving rape within marriage in a Muslim family appeared before the Court, it applied the *Cohen* decision, disregarding the fact that that decision was based on the personal law of the couple involved.[75]

At the time that the *Cohen* decision was delivered, several states in Australia were involved in legislative initiatives to remove the protection accorded to husbands accused of sexual assault within the marriage. The editor of the *Australian Law Journal* who became aware of the Israeli judgment, reacted enthusiastically:

> It is supremely ironical that the newly contemplated State's legislation... merely echoes after thousands of years the age-old doctrine of rabbinical law that aggressive sexual assaults by a husband on his wife are prohibited.[76]

Over a decade later the House of Lords handed down a decision in line with that of the Israeli court.[77] Their Lordships were aware of the Israeli judgment as it had been referred to by an English Law Commission shortly before the House

71. Official Gazette, First Supp., 652.

72. *See* Section 11a of the Law and Administration Ordinance, 5708—1948, I.R. [*Iton Rishmi*—Official Gazette during the tenure of the Provisional Council of State] No. 2 (1948), 1 *LSI* 7.

73. F.H. [Further Hearing] 37/80, *Cohen v. The State of Israel*, 35(1) P.D. 371, 373, *per* Cohn J.

74. *Cf.* Y. Shachar, 'Lawfully Raped', (1982) 8 *Iyunei Mishpat* (Tel-Aviv University Law Review), 649, 689-691 (*Heb.*).

75. Unreported case of the District Court of Be'er-Sheba.

76. Note, 'A Wife's Right to Say "No"', (1981) 55 *Australian Law Journal* 59, 60.

77. *R. v. R.*, [1991]4 All ER 481.

of Lords' decision.[78] Moreover, the House of Lords used language which resembles that of Maimonides: '[M]arriage is in modern times no longer one in which the wife must be the subservient chattel of the husband'.[79] It seems, therefore, that Maimonides has influenced the legal approach to rape within marriage both in Australian and English law,[80] and indirectly in other legal systems.[81]

* * *

In 1970 the Israeli Military Court in Gaza convicted a person of commiting an act of terror which cost several lives. The Court was asked to impose capital punishment in accordance with its authority under the Defence (Emergency) Regulations, 1945[82] promulgated during the British Mandate and maintained in force in Gaza under prevailing Egyptian law.[83] The Court declined to make this order, declaring:

> The Military Court is one of the judicial arms of the State of Israel. Therefore, although it has the authority to impose capital punishment, the moral concepts of the Jewish heritage of the State must serve us as a guideline. In our heritage a *Sanhedrin* [the Supreme Court in ancient Israel] that had imposed capital punishment was named 'a murderous court'.[84]

Twenty years later the Military Court in the West Bank followed this decision.[85] Further, the court quoted a *responsum* from the eleventh century providing that when handing down a verdict, the judge must be moderate,

---

78. *Law Commission Working Papers* No. 116: *Rape Within Marriage* 126 (1990).

79. N. 77 above, at 484 *per* Lord Keith.

80. Since the publication in the *Australian Law Journal*, all the Australian States have removed the common law defense.

81. For the American approach, which is by far inferior to the *Cohen* formula, *see* J.E. Hasday, 'Contest and Consent: A Legal History of Marital Rape', (2000) 88 *California Law Review*, forthcoming.

82. P.G. [The Palestine Gazette], Supp. 2, 1055.

83. Egyptian law was preserved in Gaza by virtue of the Law and Administration Ordinance Proclamation (Gaza Strip and Northern Sinai Region) (No. 2), 5727-1967, *Proclamation, Orders and Announcements of the Headquarters of the IDF Forces in the Gaza Strip and Northern Sinai Region*, p. 4. For an English translation, *see* (1971) 1 *IYHR*. 421.

84. Gaza 652/70, unreported.

85. Ramallah 3009/89, *The Military Prosecutor v. Takruro*, unreported, abridged in 25 *HaLishka* 33 (1995) (*Heb.*).

reconsider the matter and remove all anger from his heart, lest the desire to take revenge divert him from 'the good and right path'.[86]

* * *

In 1920, a vineyard worker from Rishon Le'zion who had been dismissed from his employment, sued his employer before the District Jewish Court of Arbitration (*Mishpat Ha'Shalom Ha'Ivri*) in Jaffa. These Courts were established in 1909 by the Office of the Zionist Organization and resumed operation after the British were granted a Mandate over Palestine. These Courts functioned as arbitration tribunals and purported to revive and renew Jewish law as a national law.[87] The worker, who at the time of his dismissal was 64 years old, sued his employer for 'a steady salary which would suffice for his family's living'. The Court rejected his suit on the grounds that only the legislature could introduce compulsory pensions, but nonetheless ordered the employer to pay the employee compensation equivalent to a month's salary for each year the plaintiff had worked for him. The Court based its decision on 'the custom accepted in the country to pay a month's compensation to a worker who had been dismissed after a year's work'.[88]

Indeed, in a restatement of Hebrew labour law published in 1942, it was stated that:

> It is an accepted and absolute custom among Jewish workers in Eretz Israel that in the case of every worker, employee and permanent official who is dismissed by an employer, the employer is obliged to give compensation to the person dismissed of a month for every year that he worked for him, a month per year according to the amount of the wage of the last month prior to his dismissal.[89]

---

86. *Responsa Rashba*, Part 5, 238 [a].

87. For the Jewish Courts of Arbitration, *see* Elon, *Jewish Law*, n. 12 above, 1532-96; P. Dykan (Dickshtein), *History of the Jewish Court of Arbitration* (Tel Aviv, Yavneh, 1964) (*Heb.*); P. Dykan (Dickshtein), *The Jewish Court of Arbitration—Its Theoretical and Practical Problems* (Tel Aviv, The Supreme Jewish Court of Arbitration, 1925) (*Heb.*).

88. District Court of Jaffa, Case No. 162; approved by the Supreme Court of Arbitration, Case No. 93; *see* M. Wager & P. Dickshtein, *Compensation for Dismissal: A Chapter in the Development of Labour Law in the New Jewish Settlement of Palestine* (Jerusalem, 1940), 45-48 (*Heb.*).

89. S.B. Bar-Adon, Book of Labour Laws: Collection of Laws and Customs in Work and Employer Relations (Haifa, 1942) 24 (*Heb.*).

The custom referred to by the Court had Biblical foundations. It had its roots in the command not to let a Hebrew released slave go away empty handed but to 'furnish him liberally out of thy flock, and out of thy threshingfloor, and out of thy winepress'.[90] The Jewish Courts of Arbitration consistently applied the duty to pay compensation to a worker upon the termination of work relations. In contrast, British judges dismissed similar claims on the grounds that such custom had not been proved 'beyond any reasonable doubt' to be 'the creation of a long established uniform practice, accepted by the public of its own free will'.[91] After the establishment of the State of Israel, the Supreme Court consistently recognized the practice. Finally, the *Knesset* intervened and enacted the Severance Pay Law, 5723-1963,[92] which imposed a duty to give severance pay to a worker who is dismissed after one year of continual employment. Introducing the Bill the Minister of Labour praised this right as 'the first social right that the worker in this country has achieved... in continuation of the ancient Jewish tradition'.[93]

These three precedents serve as instructive examples of the impact of Jewish teachings on the Israeli legal system. These ramifications are natural given that Jewish law is the national legal system of the Jewish people. Moreover, Jewish principles serve as positive sources of Israeli law. Thus, under the provisions of the Foundations of Law, 5740-1980[94] the courts are referred to 'the principles of freedom, justice, equity and peace of Israel's heritage', whenever a legal question arises to which the court finds no answer in statute law, case-law or by analogy. The referral to Jewish principles was re-emphasized in 1992, with the enactment of Basic Law: Human Dignity and Freedom[95]

90. *Deuteronomy* 15:14. *See* M. Elon, *Jewish Law* n. 12 above, II 924-26; IV 1631-34; and P. Dickshtein, 'Compensation for Dismissal', in *Korengreen Book, Articles in Research of the Bible in memory of Y.P. Korengreen*, (A. Vizer and B. Z. Luria (eds.), Tel-Aviv, 1964), 275, 276-281 (*Heb.*).

91. *Cohen v. Copun*, 7 P.L.R. [Palestine Law Reports] 80, 88 (1940).

92. 5723-1963 *S.H.* [*Sefer HaHukim* = the official publication of Israel's primary legislation]136; 17 *LSI* 161.

93. *D.K.* [*Divrey ha'Knesset* = Records of the *Knesset*] 33 (1962) 1050; *see also* M. Elon, *Jewish Law* n. 12 above, 1367-1370.

94. 5740-1890 *S.H.* 163; 34 *LSI* 181.

95. 5752-1992 *S.H.*, 150. For an unofficial translation see (1992) 26 *ILR* 248. This translation is not used in this article.

and Basic Law: Freedom of Occupation.[96] Both Basic Laws include 'purpose' clauses. Section 1A of Basic Law: Human Dignity and Freedom provides:

> The purpose of this Basic Law is to protect human dignity and freedom in order to anchor in a Basic Law the values of the State of Israel as a Jewish and democratic State.

A similar provision appears in section 2 of Basic Law: Freedom of Occupation. The limitation clause[97] provides:

> There shall be no violation of rights under this Basic Law except by a Law befitting the values of the State of Israel, enacted for a proper purpose, and to an extent no greater than required...

It has been decided by the Supreme Court that 'the values of the State of Israel', in the limitation clause are identical to 'the values of the State of Israel as a Jewish and democratic State', which are specified in the purpose clause.[98]

It would be wrong to suppose that Jewish principles have significance only for the Jewish people and within the State of Israel, just as it would be wrong to suppose that only Jews follow the teachings of the Bible. We have already seen the indirect influence of the Jewish approach to rape within marriage on the legal systems of Australia and England. The influence of Jewish law is even more direct.

On 17 October 1718 a 'congregation', summoned by the vice-chancellor of the University of Cambridge, decided to deprive Dr. Richard Bentley of his academic degrees in accordance with its authority under a custom from 'time out of mind'. The congregation's decision followed a decision by the vice-chancellor to suspend Dr. Bentley upon the latter's refusal to appear before him in connection with a monetary suit which had been brought against Bentley before the vice-chancellor. Dr. Bentley was not summoned to the congregation's hearings and it did not rehear the matter.

In *mandamus* hearings before the King's Bench, the congregation's proceedings were declared illegal for want of summons on the grounds that 'surely he

96. 5752-1992 *S.H.*, 114. For an unofficial translation see (1992) 26 *ILR* 247. This Basic Law was replaced in 1994, 5754-1994 *S.H.*, 90.

97. Section 8 of Basic Law: Human Dignity and Freedom and Section 4 of Basic Law: Freedom of Occupation.

98. A. Maoz, 'The Values of a Jewish and Democratic State', (1995) 19 *Iyunei Mishpat* 547, 552 (*Heb.*).

could never be deprived without notice' of his academic degrees.[99] Of interest is Fortescue J.'s reasoning:

> The laws of God and man both give the party an opportunity to make his defence, if he has any. I remember to have heard it observed by a very learned man upon such an occasion, that even God himself did not pass sentence upon Adam, before he was called upon to make his defence. Adam (says God) where art thou? Hast thou not eaten of the tree, whereof I commanded thee that thou shouldst not eat? And the same question was put to Eve also.[100]

* * *

Across the ocean, in the celebrated *Miranda* case,[101] Chief Justice Earl Warren relied expressly on Jewish law, as pronounced by Maimonides, in establishing the privilege against self-incrimination. In an effort to prove the antiquity of this privilege, Warren wrote, 'We sometimes forget how long it has taken to establish the privilege against self-incrimination, the sources from which it came and the fervour with which it was defended.' 'Its roots', explains Warren, 'go back into ancient times'.[102] In a footnote, Chief Justice Warren elaborates:

> Thirteenth century commentators found an analogue to the privilege based on the Bible. 'To sum up the matter, the principle that no man is to be declared guilty on his own admission is a divine decree'. Maimonides, *Mishneh Torah* (Code of Jewish Law), Book of Judges, Laws of the *Sanhedrin*, c. 18, par. 6, 3 *Yale Judaism Series* 52-53.[103]

Distinguishing the *Bentley* decision from the *Miranda* case is the fact that the English judges referred to a Biblical source whereas Chief Justice Warren

---

99. *R. v. The Chancellor, Masters and Scholars of the University of Cambridge*, 1 Srange 557, 566; 93 E.R. 698, 703.

100. *Ibid.*, at 567 (704).

101. *Miranda v. Arizona*, 384 U.S. 436 (1966).

102. *Ibid.*, 458.

103. *Ibid* n. 27. Chief Justice Warren also refers to N. Lamm, 'The Fifth Amendment and its Equivalent in *Halacha*', (1950) 3 *Judaism* 53, also established in 17 Decalogue, Four (Jan-Feb., 1967) 1. References to the *Halachic* approach to the issue of self incrimination may also be found in *Garrity v. New Jersey*, 385 U.S. 493, 497-98, n.5, (1967); *Younie v. Maryland*, 272 Md. 233, 322 A.2d. 211 (1974); *New Jersey v. McCloskey*, 90 N.J. 18; *New York v. Jo-Anne Brown*, 86 M.2d. 339.

expressly referred to *Halachic* law.[104] It is indeed necessary to distinguish between references to the Old Testament and Jewish law.[105] But the matter is not as simple as it would appear. While Fortescue J. referred to the story in *Genesis*, he relied on a Jewish classical interpretation of the Biblical verse, for this is what Don Yitzhak Abarbanel, one of the greatest commentators on the Bible, inferred from the verse from *Genesis*:

> And He taught us, Blessed Be He, that it is not appropriate for the judge to try a person, if he does not hear his version. Because God Blessed Be He, while knowing the mysteries of the heart, did not punish him [Adam] till he listened to his arguments.[106]

Similarly, one of the leading *Halachic* authorities, Rabbi Moses Isserles, known by his acronym 'Rema', wrote in his *responsa*:[107]

---

104. Though Chief Justice Warren speaks of 'an analogue to the privilege grounded in the Bible' (n. 99 above), he refers to Maimonides. Moreover, 'the Pentateuch is silent on the role of the criminal confession', (A. Kirshenbaum, *Self- Incrimination in Jewish Law* (New York, 1970) 32), and the exclusionary rule is laid down by 'Talmudic or Rabbinic law', (G. Horowitz, 'The Privilege Against Self-Incrimination—How Did it Originate?' (1957-1958) 31 *Temple Law Quarterly*, 121, 125). The Judaic foundations of this privilege in Anglo-American law are controversial. The opponents of such *nexus* stress the different scope and background of the rule disqualifying confessions in criminal cases in Anglo-American and Jewish law (*see e.g.* A. Enker, 'Self-Incrimination in Jewish Law (An Essay)', *Dine Israel*, CVII, *see also* Kirshenbaum above). Others point to the fact that John Lilburn, whose trial served as a landmark in establishing the privilege, raised in his defence 'the laws of God', and the practice of the High Priest in trying Jesus Christ (3 How. St. Tr. 1315 (1637)). It was suggested, therefore, that the privilege had its origin in Jewish law (S. Mandelbaum, 'The Privilege Against Self-Incrimination in Anglo-American and Jewish Law',(1956) 5 *The American Journal of Comparative Law*, 118, 119). Another writer attributes the Jewish foundations of the privilege to the works of the seventeenth century Hebraists of England and to the revolt of the Puritans against compulsory self-incrimination practiced under Canon law (G. Horowitz, above, 136-143). Another writer further points out a development in United States law relating to the privilege against self-incrimination—from exclusion of confessions obtained by coercion likely to produce unreliable confessions to a stage 'very close to an absolute law on extra-judicial confessions', an absolutism which underlines the Judaic attitude (M. Halbserstam, 'The Rationale For Excluding Incriminating Statements: U.S. Law Compared to Ancient Jewish Law' in *Jewish Law and Current Legal Problems* (N. Rakover (ed.), Jerusalem, 1984) 177, 185.

105. *See* D.A. Ashburn, 'Appealing to a Higher Authority?' n. 53 above.

106. *Abarbanel on the Torah, Genesis* 3:9.

107. *Responsa Rema*, 108.

> It is obvious that one cannot adjudicate in a matter without hearing the defendant's argument, since the *Torah* said: '[And I charged your judges at that time] hear the causes between your bretheren [and judge righteously between every man and his brother, and the stranger that is with him'. (*Deuteronomy*, 1:16).
> And though this is obvious, we might learn from the paths of God Blessed Be He, whose paths are just and whose ways are pleasant. He approached Adam and asked: 'Who told thee that thou wast naked? Hast thou not eaten of the tree, whereof I commanded thee that thou shouldst not eat?. And the man said...'
> Likewise, the Lord said unto Cain: 'Where is Abel thy brother?' And he said: 'I know not'... And [the Lord] said: 'What hast thou done?' in order to hear his arguments. The more so, a layman [*i.e.* a human judge].
> The Sages have given a similar interpretation. From what was said [by God following the events of Sodom and Gomorrah]: 'I will go down now, and see whether they have done altogether according to the cry of it.' (*Genesis* 18:21) 'He taught the judges not to judge until they have heard and understood.' The conclusion is that even if it is clear to the judge that the defendant is guilty, he must first hear his arguments.

Referring to this issue, the Deputy President of the Supreme Court of Israel, Justice Elon, held that 'the right to argue and be heard in Court originates and is based in the heritage of Israel from time immemorial, and the Sages of Israel saw it as the earliest basic right in human culture.' Justice Elon added:

> As the right to be heard is a basic right in the legal system in Israel, it is right and proper that this right be implemented in every place where an Israeli authority acts and functions, even if the laws applicable in that place—whether domestic or public international laws—do not require such implementation. Silence on the part of domestic law and public international law regarding this right is not in the nature of a negative arrangement.[108]

Indeed, the Supreme Court applied the right to be heard to the activities of the armed forces in the territories administered by Israel, notwithstanding that no provision is made for this right either in the law applicable to the territories by virtue of which the civil administration operated or in international law.[109] In fact, Israel is the only country in the history of international law which has opened the doors of its courts before the petitions of residents

---

108. H.C. [High Court] 4112/90, *The Association for Civil Rights in Israel v. Commander of the Southern District*, 44(4) P.D. 626, 637; 23 (1993) *IYHR* 333.

109. G. von Glahn, *The Occupation of Enemy Territory: A Commentary on the Law and Practice of Belligerent Occupation* (Minneapolis, 1957) 108.

of occupied territories against the actions of the occupying military forces.[110] The rationale for this is similar to that of the military courts in the territories in refraining from imposing capital punishment:

> Indeed, the rules of Israeli law have not been made applicable to the region, however, an Israeli official in the area carries with his office the duty to behave in accordance with the additional standards required by the fact that he is an Israeli authority, wherever the place of its activity... An official, generally, does not meet his obligations if he only acts as required by the norms of international law, because, as an Israeli authority more is required from him, and this is because he should also act in an area under military government in accordance with the rules laying out fair and proper administrative processes.[111]

An interesting point in this context relates to the post-Biblical sources of *Halacha*. These draw their authority from Biblical law itself and see themselves only as interpreters of it. Nonetheless, under the guise of interpretation, the Sages have occasionally modified Biblical law to the extent of even reaching opposite conclusions. Reference was made above to the refusal of the Military Court in Gaza and the West Bank to impose capital punishment. The Court based its decision on 'the moral concepts of Jewish heritage',[112] yet a review of the *Torah* reveals that the death penalty was commonly applied in Biblical times. Referring to this issue, Haim Cohn wrote:[113] 'The question whether capital punishment can qualify as a Jewish value is, in view of its many Biblical instances, generally answered in the affirmative'. Indeed, Maimonides lists thirty-nine offences for which a court is ordered to impose capital punishment.[114]

---

110. *Amnesty International Report, 1984*, p. 84; E. Nathan, 'The Power of Supervision of the High Court of Justice over Military Government' in M. Shamgar (ed.) *Military Government in the Occupied Territories Administered by Israel, 1967-1986: The Legal Aspects*, vol. 1 (Jerusalem, 1982) 450; A. Maoz. 'Defending Civil Liberties Without a Constitution—The Israeli Experience', (1988) 16 *Melbourne University Law Review* 815, 824.

111. H.C. 64, 493/81 *Abu Ita v. The Commander of Jerusalem and Samaria Region*, 37(2) P.D. 197, 231; abridged in (1983) 18 *Israel Law Review* 475.

112. Text accompanying n. 80 above.

113. H. Cohn, 'Capital Punishment—A Jewish Value', (1999) 1 *Democratic Culture* 37 (*Heb.*). The quotations here are from the English abstract, at p.p. 10-11.

114. *Maimonides, Hilchot Sanhedrin*, 15:10-13.

Nevertheless, adds Cohn, 'the true Jewish value now is the abolition of capital punishment'. This is so, as 'in *Talmudic* law, ways and means were deliberately sought, and actually found, to render capital punishment nugatory'.

Obviously, the Sages could not abolish capital punishment imposed by the *Torah*. However, they achieved this end by laying down several requirements which made it impossible to carry out Biblical law, while at the same time basing these requirements on the Bible itself. This technique is described by Cohn as follows:

> [F]or capital punishment to be imposed under Biblical law by the courts, it was laid down that no person was to be tried and convicted of a capital crime... unless it was first established, by the testimony of at least two competent witnesses, that they had, immediately before the commission of the criminal act, given the offender a specific warning to the effect that what he was about to do was a criminal offence, that the capital punishment provided for that offence would be carried out in such and such a fashion, and that he would do better to abstain from carrying his intention into effect. That warning, however, was useless, unless the would-be offender replied that he had understood it, and that he was proceeding to act nevertheless, even if he would have to suffer that particular capital punishment.

In concluding this issue, Cohn writes:

> This procedure is shown to be wholly illusory; and it is submitted that it was designed as a well-nigh infallible means to prevent capital punishment from ever being executed. Without abrogating, formally or at all, any Biblical law, the Sages merely put in the way of capital trials such insurmountable obstacles as would suffice to accomplish their purpose.[115]

Similarly, it is agreed that the legal institution of employee severance pay is rooted in the Biblical law relating to the gratuity that the Hebrew slave is entitled to receive when he obtains his freedom. Nevertheless, '[t]he *Halachic* authorities found in this law the concept of giving a certain sum to an employee at the termination of his employment.'[116] No specific obligation to provide severance pay is to be found in the Bible. As explained by Professor Elon '[t]he inference from the law of the Hebrew slave to the law of an employee was possible because under Jewish law the status of a Hebrew

---

115. For an analysis of the approach of Judaism to capital punishment, *see* D. Di-Sola, 'Capital Punishment Among the Jews', in (1916) *Jewish Eugenics and Other Essays*, 51.

116. *Ibid.*

slave is comparable to the status of an employee'.[117] To use Philo's expression, '[f]or people in this position, though we find them called slaves, are in reality labourers'.[118]

G. Epilogue

Yeshayahu Leibowitz, one of the most famous Jewish thinkers of the present age, emphasized an inherent contradiction between Judaism, as a religion, on one hand, and humanism and morality as civil phenomena, on the other. In his view:

> No social, political or economic program could be derived from Judaism. Judaism does not engage in social or in human problems as such. This is so because man is meaningless... there is no intrinsic value in man himself but only in his position before God. Judaism is not humanism... The social constitution of the *Torah* is neither social nor philanthropic: it does not stem from the concept of human rights but rather from man's duty.[119]

In Leibowitz' opinion:

> The attempt to fuse morality and religion is not a happy one... Judaism did not produce an ethical theory of its own, was never embodied in a moral system, and made no pretence of representing a specific moral point of view.[120]

Leibowitz' approach is that of the believer who adheres to the precepts of religion merely because it is God's will. Under this approach the moral basis of religious precepts should be totally irrelevant. Leibowitz' approach touches upon fundamental philosophical dilemmas concerning the relationship between religion and morality and between divine supremacy and human autonomy, which have engaged theologians and philosophers since the beginning of civilization. This is not the proper place to deal with these dilemmas.[121] Suffice it to mention that Leibowitz was sharply criticized from even a

---

117. *Ibid.*, 925.

118. *Philo: With an English translation by F.H. Colson*, 11 vols. (London, 1937) VII, 357.

119. Y. Leibowitz, *Judaism, Jewish People and the State of Israel* 310 (Jerusalem, 1975) (*Heb.*).

120. *Ibid.*, at 6-7.

121. For a comprehensive discussion of these issues, *see* D. Statman & A. Sagi, *Religion and Morality* (Jerusalem, 1993) (*Heb.*).

religious point of view.[122] Leibowitz' philosophy is unique in Jewish religious thought and he was accused of entertaining a superficial and one-dimensional perception of the essence of Judaism.[123] Yet, even if sound from a religious point of view, this perception is irrelevant to the thesis advocated in this article. In the opinion of Leibowitz, 'the religious end is the ultimate end' and 'is desecrated when it is made to serve as a means to some other end'.[124] In his view 'a person acting as a moral agent cannot be acting as a religious agent.' This is so since 'human actions... can only be identified in terms of the agent's intention.' Therefore, 'a religious action cannot be simultaneously a moral action.'[125] Leibowitz stresses the idea that '[t]he Bible does not recognize the good and the right as such, only "the good and the right in the eyes of God"'.[126] Yet, the real question is whether that which is good and right in the eyes of God is also good and right from a moral point of view. I have tried to show throughout this article that fundamentally this is so.

Speaking of 'the character of God', Moore wrote:

> God's justice is first of all man's assurance that God will not use His almighty power over His creatures without regard to right.[127]

It is, moreover, disputable whether what is 'good and right in the eyes of God' is the ultimate good even in the eyes of the Bible. The Bible records several episodes where the acts of God were challenged from a moral point of view. Thus, when God informed Abraham of his decision to destroy Sodom and

---

122. For criticism of Leibowitz, *see Negation for Negation's Sake: Versus Yeshayahu Leibowitz—Essays and Comments* (Ch. Ben-Yerucham & Ch. E. Kolitz (eds.), Jerusalem, El-HaShorashim, 1983) (*Heb.*); M. Granot, *A Singular Faith* (Tel Aviv, 1993) (*Heb.*); M. Gilboa, *Y. Leibowitz: Ideas and Contradictions* (Sede Boker: The Ben-Gurion Research Center, 1994) (*Heb.*).

123. *See* A. Sagi, 'The Punishment of Amalek: The Ways Jewish Tradition Competes With the Moral Issue and the Status of Morality in the Jewish Tradition' in *Multiculturalism in a Democratic and Jewish State* (M. Mautner, A. Sagi and R. Shamir (eds.), Tel-Aviv, 1998), 477, 509 (*Heb.*); L. Jacobs, 'The Relationship Between Religion and Ethics in Jewish Thought', in *Contemporary Jewish Ethics* (M.M. Kellner (ed.), New York, 1978), 41.

124. E. Goldman in his Introduction to Y. Leibowitz, *Judaism, Human Values and the Jewish State*, (Cambridge: E. Goldman, ed. & trans., 1992), xvi.

125. *Ibid. See also* Statman & Sagi, n. 111 above, Ch. 7.

126. N. 119 above, at 7, quoting from *Deuteronomy* 12:28.

127. N. 47 above, vol. I, at 387-88.

Gomorrah as an act of retaliation for the sins of the inhabitants of these cities, Abraham reprimanded 'the Judge of all the earth' for failing to do justice.[128] Furthermore, it has been suggested that Judaism recognizes the autonomy of morality and accords it religious value.[129] Yet, even if we disregard this well reasoned model, it is hard to accept Leibowitz' attempt to divorce Judaism from morality and deny it any social mission.

We have encountered an episode where God's ruling was overruled by the Sages and he was defeated.[130] This does not derogate from God's supremacy as it was he who laid down the rule that 'after the majority must one incline'.[131] Yet, as explained by Justice Silberg,[132] this episode does subject God, like human beings, to the rule of law. Moreover, the fact that God instituted the majority rule may indicate that God does not act arbitrarily, but rather is led by moral considerations. The morality of God and its direct impact on human behaviour is vividly demonstrated in a *midrash* included in the *Babylonian Talmud*. The Biblical verse: 'Ye shall walk after the Lord your God'[133] is interpreted in the *Talmud* as follows:

> What means the text?.. Is it then possible for a human being to walk after the *Shechinah* [the Divine Presence]; for has it not been said 'For the Lord thy God is a consuming fire'? (*Deuteronomy* 4:24) But [the meaning is] to walk after the attributes of the Holy One, Blessed Be He. As He clothed the naked..., so do thou also clothe the naked. The Holy One, Blessed Be He, visited the sick..., so do thou also visit the sick. The Holy One, Blessed Be He, comforted mourners..., so do thou also comfort mourners. The Holy One, Blessed Be He, buried the dead..., so do thou also bury the dead. (Tractate *Sotah* 14a).

At the end of this brief survey of Judaic teachings it is submitted that Judaism does indeed play a central role in advancing human rights. One may ask why it should matter whether Judaism propounds the preservation of human rights. The answer is that the doctrine of human rights is still fragile. It cannot exist

---

128. *Genesis* 18:25.

129. *See*, A. Sagi, *Judaism: Between Religion and Morality* (Tel-Aviv, 1998) (*Heb.*); L. Jacobs, 'The Relationship Between Religion and Ethics in Jewish Thought', in *Religion and Morality* (G. Outka and J.P. Reeder (eds.), 1973).

130. Text accompanying n. 44 above.

131. Text accompanying n. 43 above.

132. Text accompanying n. 45 above.

133. *Deuteronomy* 13:4.

in the abstract divested of social concepts. Religion plays a major role in society, Jewish ideas and values have infused western culture directly and have had an indirect impact through Christianity, enriching western humanistic and liberal thinking. Jewish ideas and values are capable of enriching it still further.

Perceptions of the Other—Lessons from Jewish-Christian Dialogue

Edward Kessler*

If we take the twentieth century as our starting point it is quite clear that two immense events have combined to provide a dual focus to Jewish-Christian Dialogue today:

– The Holocaust (Shoah)
– The Creation of the State of Israel

Both spurred an intense desire amongst many Christians and Jews to learn about the history, theology and other aspects of Jewish-Christian Relations. The Shoah resulted in a general awareness of the immensity of the burden which the Church carried not only for its general silence, with some noble exceptions during 1933-45, but also because of the 'teaching of contempt' towards Jews and Judaism which it carried on for so many centuries. As Jules Isaac showed immediately after the war, it was this that sowed the seeds of hatred and made it so easy for Hitler to use antisemitism as a political weapon.

* Founding and Executive Director of the Centre for Jewish-Christian Relations at Cambridge (www.cjcr.cam.ac.uk).

Raphael Walden (ed.), Racism and Human Rights, *85-100.*

Although no one would deny that Nazism was opposed to Christianity, it is well known that Hitler often justified his antisemitism with reference to the Church and Christian attitudes towards Judaism.

As a result of the soul searching that took place after 1945, many Christians began the painful process of re-examining the sources of the teaching of contempt and repudiating them. Christian institutions, most notably the Vatican, the World Council of Churches and individual Protestant denominations have, since then, issued declarations against the perpetuation of this teaching.

This meant from a Christian perspective that before dialogue could take place the history of the Church and its attitude towards the Jews had to be publicly acknowledged. This involved a proper appraisal of antisemitism, anti-Judaism and the significance of the Shoah. If we take the Roman Catholic Church and the Second Vatican Council (1962-5) as an example, the publication *Nostra Aetate* ('In Our Time') marked the beginnings of a fresh approach. The Roman Catholic Church 'came in from out of the cold' and rejected the millennial teaching of contempt of Jews and Judaism and unequivocally asserted the Church's debt to its Jewish heritage. Most importantly of all, it ushered in a new era, fresh attitudes, a new language of discourse never previously heard in the Catholic Church concerning Jews. The concept of a dialogue now entered the Jewish-Christian relationship.

More recent Christian institutional statements have consistently condemned antisemitism and documents such as the Roman Catholic Document, *We Remember*, illustrate a willingness to tackle this subject. Most Christian theologians involved in Jewish-Christian dialogue acknowledge that the slaughter of 6,000,000 Jews would not have been possible were the roots of antisemitism not deep within the Christian tradition.

Another example of the changes can be seen in the repudiation of the teachings of Martin Luther by the Lutheran World Federation, which rejected 'Luther's violent invective against the Jews and express deep and abiding sorrow over its tragic effects on subsequent generations'. In particular, it deplored the appropriation of Luther's words by modern antisemites and called for increasing Lutheran-Jewish cooperation.

Documents such as these are directed to a Christian public and are primarily a sincere call for the renunciation of antisemitism. They reach not only Christians in Western Europe and North America, where dialogue has progressed, but also Christians in regions such as Eastern Europe, Africa, Asia and Latin America where many have never encountered a Jew. Thus, **as far**

as antisemitism is concerned, the Protestant Churches and the Roman Catholic Church instead of being part of the problem have now become part of the solution.

Unfortunately, the same is not true of the Orthodox Church. The changes that have taken place in what may be described as the Western churches find few parallels in the East. Despite a few interfaith meetings, and despite some bold statements by a few Orthodox leaders, there is simply no comparison with the current state of play in the Roman Catholic and Protestant churches. Much has to be done before Orthodox Christianity abandons its repository of anti-Jewish polemic.

The Shoah not only caused Christianity to reassess its relationship with Judaism but also stirred greater Jewish interest in Christianity. Jonathan Sacks spoke for many when he stated that, 'today we meet and talk together because we must; because we have considered the alternative and seen where it ends and we are shocked to the core by what we have seen'.

The need to tackle such issues as the Shoah in Jewish-Christian dialogue is self-evident but there are dangers if they are not conducted in perspective. Fackenheim's proclamation that the Shoah resulted in a new commandment, the 614th, which stressed that it was incumbent upon Jews to survive as Jews, is a case in point. According to Fackenheim one remained a Jew so as not to provide Hitler a posthumous victory. However, as a result, Jewish identity became Shoah centred and, at the same time, Jewish-Christian dialogue became Shoah centred. The danger is that by focusing solely on the Holocaust Jews and Christians will gain a distorted view. For example, a young Jew will construct a negative Jewish identity, which without the positive side of Judaism, will not be a value to be handed down over the generations. A young Christian will come away with an exclusive picture of the Jew as victim without an awareness of the positive aspects of Jewish culture.

It is a result of the emphasis on Shoah and antisemitism that Jewish-Christian dialogue has often appeared to consist of an attempt to educate Christians about Judaism in order to prevent, or at the very least, to reduce Christian antisemitism. Thus, Jews and Christians become involved in dialogue on account of defensive factors, in other words, to stop the possibility of antisemitism from breaking out in churches in the future. Although Jewish-Christian dialogue proceeds at many levels and reaction to the Shoah is an important driving force, dialogue cannot be built solely on responses to antisemitism and Christian feelings of guilt. Indeed, no healthy and enduring relationship between people is built on guilt. If recent Christian soul-searching in the aftermath of the destruction of European Jewry leads to a new approach and a revision of traditional anti-Jewish teaching so much the better. However, the future relationship cannot be built on the foundations of guilt. The sense of guilt is transient and does not pass to the next generation; moreover, it is unstable and inherently prone to sudden and drastic reversal.

This is acknowledged in *Dabru Emet* ('Speak Truth'), a broad-based Jewish statement about the relationship with Christianity. *Dabru Emet* is the first detailed modern cross-denominational document examining the place of Christianity in Jewish thought. Issued in September 2000, *Dabru Emet* stressed it was time for Jews to reflect on what Judaism may now say about Christianity. It comments on the Shoah, assessing Christian guilt while separating Christianity from Nazism:

> Nazism was not a Christian phenomenon. Without the long history of Christian anti-Judaism and Christian violence against Jews, Nazi ideology could not have taken hold nor could it have been carried out... But Nazism itself was not an inevitable outcome of Christianity... We encourage the continuation of recent efforts in Christian theology to repudiate unequivocally contempt of Judaism and the Jewish people. We applaud those Christians who reject this teaching of contempt, and we do not blame them for the sins committed by their ancestors.

This passage has been criticised by some for having gone too far; others were troubled to learn that some Jews do view Nazism as the logical outcome of European Christian culture and some expressed concern that Christians might feel completely exonerated by the Jewish statement. Most importantly of all, perhaps, is the fact that the statement illustrates that dialogue needs to move onto a more positive basis.

The second key issue in Jewish-Christian dialogue is the establishment of the State of Israel. There is little doubt that whilst the Church has for many years been grappling with issues related to Christian antisemitism, attitudes towards the Land and State of Israel have, from the theological perspective, proved more difficult to tackle. Theological difficulties have made a Christian re-orientation to Israel problematic. Simply put, it has been easier for Christians to condemn antisemitism as a misunderstanding of Christian teaching than to come to terms with the re-establishment of the Jewish State. As a result, the subject of Israel has probably caused as much disagreement and division within the Church as any other topic in Jewish-Christian dialogue.

The Christian reluctance to accept the implications of the new State in the Jewish-Christian relationship has only served to reinforce its centrality in discussion. In addition, its significance lies in the fact that, first, Israel is the only State in which Jews form the majority and this has important consequences for the Jewish–Christian relationship. For example, Jews have more confidence in their dealings with Christians. Also, most of the Christian holy places are now in Israel or in Israeli controlled territory, which means that the entire Christian world takes a close interest in developments. This has led to strong reactions—both of a favourable and unfavourable nature—but the very existence of this spotlight shining so strongly on Israel, and especially on Jerusalem, gives particular importance to any attempt at mutual understanding between Christian and Jew inside Israel.

However, there are a number of dangers with basing a theology of Jewish-Christian dialogue primarily on Israel. One is the fact that dialogue becomes linked to certain stages of achievement, which give an impression of a direct line of progress. Valuable as the stages of achievement are, they are often far from the complexities of the reality itself. There is great danger in arguing that what was once an interpretation about the nature of the biblical word and promise is now in the situation of Israel concretised in a contemporary event. The challenge to Jewish-Christian dialogue as a result of an emphasis on fulfilment of biblical prophecy can be seen in the writings of some evangelical Christians as well as fundamentalist Jews.

For example, what happened a hundred years ago to the Jews outside of Israel is considered by some as historically remote compared to biblical events, which are viewed as almost contemporary. The present becomes transformed into biblical language and geography, which leads to the danger of giving metaphysical meaning to geographical places. The fundamentalist Jew in Israel interprets the ownership of the Land of Israel in terms of a divine gift. This creates a great danger of bestowing divine importance to Israel and the vocation of the Jew becomes a dedication to the existence and the restoration of the cosmic state. Thus, the return to the Land is a fulfillment of the divine promise and reflects a return to the original fullness. However, the biblical promises do not define the same borders and by choosing the widest ones the fundamentalist abuses the idea of the promise, which is related to the Land.

The dangers of Israel-based dialogue are also illustrated by those who, in the name of dialogue, move from a position of commitment for the well being of Israel to one of almost Israel can do no wrong. This is not conducive to dialogue for it is not an honest and sober conversation firmly related to present realities.

The 1994 Vatican recognition of the State of Israel marks a significant shift in Christian thinking. Its significance is explained by David Rosen, who was intimately involved in the negotiations with the Vatican:

> This is the end of the beginning. The implications of *Nostra Aetate* and the subsequent documents called out for full relations between the Holy See and the State of Israel. Their absence had suggested that the reconciliation between the church and the Jewish People was not a complete one. Accordingly, for the last three decades, Jewish representatives have called on the Vatican to take this step. The agreement that was signed last week, therefore, has historical and philosophical importance as well as diplomatic significance. Now we can address the meaning of our relationship and get on to many other matters of common interest.

The question is what are the 'other matters of common interest' and what is their relevance to dialogue?

Understanding the Meaning of Dialogue

Having described key issues in Jewish-Christian dialogue we now move on to consider the basis for dialogue.

- How does modern interfaith dialogue differ from the interfaith disputations of the Middle Ages?
- How does inter-faith dialogue differ from the bargaining of the market in which the aim is to find a mutually acceptable compromise?

In fact modern interfaith dialogue is neither disputation nor seeking for compromise.

First, the word 'dialogue' and dialogue activity have been both misconstrued and ill-defined. A casual conversation between Jews and Christians that may add up to no more than a loose restatement of entrenched theological positions is sometimes claimed as dialogue. Any communication between persons of two differing religious points of view that does not involve a genuine hearing of the other is all too easily claimed as dialogue. Today, one can communicate with others either by phone, fax or e-mail but dialogue requires more effort, and most of all, a face to face contact. Dialogue is not simply a method of communication.

Second, the word is sloppily used as almost an umbrella term to cover a whole host of related word activities that are good in themselves, some of them even providing an essential framework for dialogue, but are not the equivalent to dialogue. For example, some adopt the term Jewish-Christian relations as synonymous with dialogue. After all you can have good or bad relations (as often the case with relatives) but relations in themselves are not the equivalent of dialogue; nor is the comparative study of religions, which is also taken by some as a synonym for dialogue. Of course, dialogue does involve the serious study of the religion of others, but the understanding required before dialogue can take place consists of more, for example, than the understanding of the major festivals and life-cycles of Judaism and Christianity.

In reality, dialogue consists of a direct meeting of two people and involves a reciprocal exposing of the full religious consciousness of the one with the 'Other'. Dialogue speaks to the Other with a full respect of what the Other is and has to say. This is never less than personal but can develop in such a way as to be extended to a group and even to communities. However, it begins with the individual and not with the community.

This is not an original definition for the biblical prophets were experts in this full personal communication and encounter. Isaiah in a famous passage powerfully commends Israel to enter into a personal relationship with God stating, 'come now let us reason together' (Isaiah 1:18). We should also refer to Leviticus 19:33-34: 'When a stranger lives with you in your land, do not ill-treat him. The stranger who lives with you shall be treated like a native-born. Love him as yourself for you were strangers in the land of Egypt. I am the Lord your God.' These verses provide the theological basis for dialogue—indeed, the command to love the stranger is found on 36 occasions in the Pentateuch. Dialogue consists of embracing the dignity of difference and is dependent upon a willingness to understand the difference and to get to know the Other.

Such a quest is never easy because it is not merely about the Other, nor where the Other differs from us. The thoughts and experience of dialogue are well expressed in the writings of Franz Rosenzweig. Rosenzweig's emphasis is not on the subject matter that connects the speaker with the listener but the I confronting the Thou. The word is not only an expression of reality but also a means by which to express it.

Speech for Rosenzweig consisted of articulating an awareness and comprehension in living contact with another person, which he called *sprachdenken*. Thus the use of words in a live encounter was for him more than just talking, in other words something is not only said but something happens. This means that dialogue is dependent upon the presence of another person. It is not difficult to see how Rosenzweig became one of the main sources out of which Martin Buber developed his 'I and Thou' formula.

Buber in his exposition of the I-Thou relationship maintained that a personal relationship with God is only truly personal when there is not only awe and respect on the human side but when we are not overcome and overwhelmed in our relationship with God. This is illustrated by a famous story found in the Talmud in which Rabbi Eliezer appeals to heaven and the voice of God declares that he is right. However, the *halakhah* (Jewish law) still follows the majority opinion (in opposition to Rabbi Eliezer) because of the principle 'it is not in heaven' (Deut. 30:12). Many years later, the story concludes, Elijah tells Rabbi Nathan that when the incident took place God laughed and declared, 'My children have conquered Me'. The significance of the story for our study lies in its presentation of the personal relationship between God and humankind.

This has implications for human-human dialogue because it means that two people must meet as two valid centres of interest. Thus one should approach the Other with respect and restraint so that the validity of the other centre is in no sense belittled. Further, not only is the essential being of the other respected but the world of faith is also treated as valid and genuine; not an 'it' to be carelessly set aside but a distinctive value of belief. An I-Thou relationship is a meeting not of religions but of religious people. The emphasis is placed on the individual.

This illustrates the foundational principle of dialogue today: understand the other as the other wishes to be understood. In terms of Jewish-Christian dialogue, this means that Judaism and Christianity must be understood on their own terms.

This has significant implications for the perception of the other because dialogue involves a respect that takes the other as seriously as one demands to be taken oneself. This is an immensely difficult and costly exercise. We find it all too easy to relate to others in a casual way with a lack of concentration on the reality and good of the Other.

Thus genuine dialogue between Christians and Jews only started when Christians showed a willingness not only to repudiate antisemitism but also to show a desire to understand Judaism as Jews understand Judaism. This process began with a reawakening to the Jewish origins of Christianity.

Christians renounced many of the triumphalist doctrines, most significantly the renunciation of the teaching of the divine rejection of the Jewish people since the time of Jesus—in other words, the divine covenant with the

Jewish people is now no longer viewed as having been annulled. According to the 1980 Evangelical Church of the Rhineland statement,

> We believe the permanent election of the Jewish people as the people of God and realize that through Jesus Christ the church is into the covenant of God with his people.

For its part, the Roman Catholic Church teaches Christians that 'the Jews remain most dear to God' who 'does not repent of the gifts He makes nor of the calls He issues'. John Paul II spelled it out in the early years of his pontificate as follows: God's covenant with the Jewish people had never been broken, retains eternal validity; God does not renege on his promises. If the Jews were not rejected, then Judaism was not a fossilized faith, as had been taught previously, but a living, authentic religion.

The ramifications were manifold. Christians were now told that Jesus, his family and his followers were Jewish and the Jewish background to Christianity was now stressed. Stated first in recent times by the 1947 Seelisburg document, Christians are commended to,

– Remember that Jesus was born of a Jewish mother of the seed of David and the people of Israel, and that His everlasting love and forgiveness embraces His own people and the whole world.
– Remember that the first disciples, the apostles and the first martyrs were Jews

The rediscovery of the Jewishness of the origins of Christianity led to Christians being taught about the richness of the Jewish context as well as to the perils of relying on the literal text of the New Testament. New subjects for consideration were also broached which included the closeness of the relationship between Jesus and the Pharisees. Catholics now learn that Jesus 'had very close relations' with the Pharisees to whom 'he was very near'.

In addition, Christian ordinands were being taught that the final text of the Gospels was edited long after the events described and, for example, that the authors were concerned with denigrating those Jews who did not follow Jesus. At the same time they were concerned with vindicating the Romans, whose goodwill they were seeking. This was courageously admitted by the Vatican's 1985 *Notes* on the teaching of Judaism, which stated forthrightly:

> It cannot be ruled out that some references hostile or less than favorable to the Jews have their historical context in conflicts between the nascent Church and the Jewish

> community. Certain controversies reflect Christian-Jewish relations long after the time of Jesus. To establish this is of capital importance if we wish to bring out the meaning of certain Gospel texts for the Christians of today.

There was a realisation that too often Christians have pictured Torah as a burden rather than as a delight. Christians were reminded that Jesus was a faithful Jew and 'that from the Jewish people sprang the apostles'. Christian re-acquaintance with Judaism resulted primarily from an increased awareness of the Jewish origins of Christianity. That Jesus was born lived and died a Jew; that the first Christians were Jews; that the New Testament is, for the most part, a Jewish work. From the Jewish side individuals such as Martin Buber and Claude Montefiore reminded Jews that Jesus was a fellow Jew (their 'great brother' as Martin Buber described him).

A Common Mission

On many major issues, therefore, Jews and Christians find themselves on the same side of the fence, faced with the same challenges. The 'perception of the other' has changed dramatically and this shift can be illustrated with a brief consideration of mission. This tenet has been, and still is, central to the Christian faith as illustrated by the legacy of the command found in the Gospels of Matthew to 'go therefore and make disciples of all nations'.

A great change has only begun to take place in the last 10 or 20 years. For instance, when the WCC was established in 1948 its first report unsurprisingly condemned antisemitism but also, perhaps incredibly when viewed in hindsight, called for a redoubling of effort at the conversion of Jews. It recommended that the churches should 'seek to recover the universality of our Lord's commission by including the Jewish people in their evangelistic work'. The conclusion of the WCC was that, in light of the Shoah, an even greater effort should be made to convert Jews. The report stated that 'because of the unique inheritance of the Jewish people, the churches should make provisions for the education of ministers specially fitted to this task. Provision should also be made for Christian literature to interpret the Gospel to Jewish people.'

Yet, here lies a dilemma for all Christians, which explains why the subject has, until recently, been avoided. Nearly all Christians agree that in their witness of Christianity they should always avoid proselytism (in the pejorative sense); they should shun all conversionary attitudes and practices which do *not* conform to the ways a free God draws free people to Himself in response to His calls to serve Him in spirit and in truth. Yet, there exists a tension. According to the Catholic theologian, Thomas Stransky:

> In the case of the Jewish people, what is Christian proselytism in practice? And what is 'evangelization'—the Church's everlasting proclamation of Jesus Christ, 'the Way, the Truth and the Life'? Is open dialogue a betrayal of Christian mission? Or is mission a betrayal of dialogue?

Interestingly, he also asks the reverse question i.e., what is the continuing mission of the synagogue to the church? What is the *common* mission of the synagogue and church?

On the one hand, Christians are taught that the Church must preach Jesus Christ to the world; on the other, they must spread their Christian faith while maintaining the strictest respect for religious liberty. Such a tension is disturbing to many Jews. For example, the belief that salvation can only come through Jesus (or through the Church) relegates not only Judaism but also all other faiths to a position of inferiority. Have the changes in doctrine starting with Vatican II robbed this belief of its former triumphalism? Some participants in the dialogue remain unconvinced and the recent publication of *Dominus Iesus* serves only to confuse rather than clarify.

However, we must remember that traditional Jewish eschatology, while not foreseeing the conversion of all to Judaism does anticipate that all nations will acknowledge the superiority and sovereignty of the God of Israel. Jews and Christians remain adherents of very different faiths and we must recognize that there are beliefs in all religions that characterize that faith and are too fundamental to compromise. This is acknowledged by *Dabru Emet* as follows:

> The humanly irreconcilable difference between Jews and Christians will not be settled until God redeems the entire world as promised in Scripture… Jews can respect Christians' faithfulness to their revelation just as we expect Christians to respect our faithfulness to our revelation. Neither Jew nor Christian should be pressed into affirming the teaching of the other community.

In 1988, at the decennial Lambeth Conference, the Anglican Communion confronted the issue of Christian mission. Unlike other gatherings, Lambeth 1988 emphasised, rather than minimised, the importance of missionary activity for Christian-Jewish relations. It re-examined the understanding of the Christian mission, which was seen not in terms of the conversion of Jews, but rather of a common mission. In the light of Christian-Jewish and Christian-Muslim relations, proselytism was to be rejected and the conference called for 'mutual witness to God between equal partners'.

It stated that although

> there are a variety of attitudes towards Judaism within Christianity today...All these approaches, however, share a common concern to be sensitive to Judaism, to reject all proselytising, that is, aggressive and manipulative attempts to convert, and of course, any hint of antisemitism. Further, Jews, Muslims and Christians have a common mission. They share a mission to the world that God's name may be honoured.

This is not to imply that there are no missionary problems today. However, there has been a dramatic downscaling of Christian mission to Jews. Instances of missionary problems come mainly from some evangelical churches (including those 'messianic' movements such as Jews for Jesus). Relations with the Evangelical Protestants are especially complex. First of all, they often do not dialogue—even with other Christians. Their fundamentalist views are not to be discussed with others (similar to fundamentalist Jews) and mission is ingrained—as was again exemplified by the recent decision of the Southern Baptist convention, one of the largest groupings in the United States, to intensify mission to the Jews in a resolution 'to direct our energies and resources toward the proclamation of the gospel to the Jewish people'.

Nevertheless, recent developments in mainstream Christian denominations illustrate another enormous shift in the Christian understanding from a mission to Israel to mission with Israel. We now encounter an emphasis on partnership and a common mission rather than the mission of Christians to Jews.

A Common Biblical Heritage

In addition to a re-evaluation of mission, another subject under review is how to approach the Bible. Both Jews and Christians claim the Scriptures—the former use the term Hebrew Bible and the latter, Old Testament. Competing claims have unsurprisingly resulted in bitter argument and negative perceptions of the other.

Today we are witnessing an increased willingness to see a multitude of different possible meanings in the interpretations of biblical texts. This is in marked contrast to the single 'authentic' meaning, backed by clerical or scholarly authority.

A Jewish justification for such an approach is found in the following passage from the Babylonian Talmud:

> In the School of Rabbi Ishmael it is taught: 'See, My word is like fire, an oracle of the Eternal, and like a hammer that shatters a rock' (Jeremiah 23:29). Just as a hammer divides into several sparks so too every scriptural verse yields several meanings.

Support for such an approach to biblical interpretation can also be found in classical Christian exegesis, such as this passage from the Syriac tradition:

> Who is capable of comprehending the extent of what is to be discovered in a single utterance ofYours? For we leave behind in it far more than we take from it, like thirsty people drinking from a fountain. The facets of His word are more numerous than the facets of those who learn from it. God depicted His word with many beauties, so that each of those who learn from it can examine that aspect of it which he likes. And God had hidden within his word all sorts of treasures, so that each of us can be enriched by it from whatever aspect he meditates on... Anyone who encounters Scripture should not suppose that the single one of its riches that he has found is the only one to exist; rather, he should realize that he himself is only capable of discovering that one out of the many riches which exist in it.

The tendency to offer a variety of different meanings, each of which claims validity, might be described in terms of *exegetical pluralism*—in other words, traditional interpretations of Scripture represent breadth and plurality of viewpoint. In this way, both the Jewish and Christian exegetical traditions provide a framework to allow for multi-various interpretations of biblical texts, which they both share. As a result, Christians and Jews may come to realise that the traditional (and sometimes negative) interpretations do not provide the final and authoritative meaning of the text.

The approach may also be adopted in the tackling of texts which run contrary to fundamental ethical values or which may be read as a license for violence or bigotry. In other words, exegetical pluralism can be applied to those texts, which have been used for much evil, as for example, the way which the Bible has been used to maintain slavery or second class citizenship, to hold women in subjugation to men, and so on.

The application of exegetical pluralism is dependent upon one criterion: that biblical interpretation should reject any interpretation, which would promote hatred, discrimination or superiority of one group over another. The use a biblical text for the purpose of the subjugation of women to men, black to white, Jew to Christian should be considered invalid, requiring reinterpretation.

This approach is justified by a hermeneutical principle shared by both Christians and Jews: humanity should live by the commandments and not die by their observance. To give two examples from rabbinic biblical interpretation:

- Deut 21:18-21 deals with the stubborn and rebellious son who is to be stoned to death. This law was turned into a purely hypothetical exercise and the command was restricted by so many conditions that it could never be applied.
- Exodus 21:24 includes the notorious 'eye for an eye' and 'tooth for a tooth'. Perhaps as early as biblical times, this was viewed a common Near-Eastern artificial construct for addressing the legal problem of damages. The 'eye for an eye' was simply applied for the discussion of compensation, as explained by Rashi, an eleventh-century French Rabbi. "If one blinded the eye of his fellow, he pays him the equivalent of the decrease of his value if he were sold in the marketplace; and similarly all of them; but it does not mean the taking of an actual limb."

Interestingly, these passages assume that because God's word could not conceivably run contrary to the highest contemporary values at any given period, the doors of interpretation are open and problematic texts can be re-interpreted so as to conform to those values. They show that whatever appeared to be a contemporary problem could be reinterpreted and effectively abolished.

The recognition that the biblical text can have more than one meaning is significant for Jewish-Christian dialogue. It is no longer essential to search for the one and only correct meaning of a text but a number of different interpretations, each within its own context, each worthy of consideration in its own right.

The existence of exegetical pluralism may leave the interpreter with an uncomfortable tension because of the presence of a number of interpretations arising out of a single biblical passage. The multitude of possible interpretations may be disconcerting but their existence illustrates a greater reality, which exists not only outside of Scripture and in society at large, but also within Scripture.

Consider the following opposing translations of Job 13:15 which highlight an inherent ambiguity within the biblical text:

- Behold, he will slay me; I have no hope (RSV)
- Though he slay me, yet will I trust in him (KJV).

The reason for the difference between the RSV and KJV is the result of a variation in the reading and spoken versions. The Masoretic vocalisation (spoken reading) indicates that Job has hope while the consonantic text (written text) offers the view that Job has no hope. The Mishnah acknowledges the ambiguous meaning of the biblical text and has recognised that both translations are possible 'the matter is undecided—do I trust in Him or not trust?' The contradiction is meaningful as it expresses the tension of one who is torn between hope and doubt: the very tension that inhabits our mind when we read the Bible today. According to Andre Neher 'Job pronounces two words which signify *simultaneously* hope and hopelessness...I hope in Him, he shouts, but also do not hope in him'.

Implementing the Changes

It is clear that many of the main divisive issues between Judaism and Christianity have been either eliminated or taken to the furthest point at which agreement is possible. The efforts of Catholics and Protestants towards respect of Judaism are reflected in documents, which project attitudes that would have been unthinkable a few decades ago. Christian theology has been profoundly revised at the official level—all Churches are committed to the fight against antisemitism and to teaching about the Jewishness of Christianity. We have seen how this has impacted upon key areas such as mission and biblical interpretation.

There is of course an important agenda for top-level dialogue and consultations but the emphasis should now shift to filtering to regional and local levels. It is possible today to respond effectively to regional requirements in the new global reality. Consciousness of the changes have been largely confined to the elite (although in certain regions, such as the United States, it has been more widely disseminated). The object now is to get these changes into the everyday understanding of all the faithful and the fields to be addressed are churches and synagogues, seminaries and *yeshivahs*, schools and universities as well as informal education, including the media.

We must ensure that the positive developments achieved are properly applied at the regional level. This means attention to education and information to ensure that the new teachings are disseminated at grass-roots levels. It involves dealing with the fight against antisemitism in regions such as Russia, certainly to combat any manifestations within a religious context.

Most importantly educational guidelines are required—designed for each region. This requirement is equally true of Jews as well as Christians. History has understandably moulded negative Christian stereotypes among Jews and we must now teach the Jewish community about the contemporary changes of attitudes by the churches. The beginnings can be seen in *Dabru Emet* but this is simply the first step. Claude Montefiore's call for a Jewish theology of Christianity over 75 years still ago waits to be answered.

The challenge of today is to harness the growing interconnectedness and interdependence of Jewish–Christian relations, supported by the revolution in information technology, which is bringing all of us closer together. We need to broaden the dialogue to include, for example, Christians from the developing world, many of whom have never encountered a Jew in their lives and know little of them except from the New Testament accounts—not always a source of positive images of Judaism.

There is no guarantee of progress. There are risks, for example, that instability in one part of the world, such as the Middle East, will effect Jewish-Christian relations in another. Giant strides have been made but we are talking of a dynamic and relentless process. We will never be able to sit back and say, 'The work is done. The agenda is completed.'

However, it is clear that we have come a long way in 50 years and Jews and Christians are more likely to share positive perceptions of the other than ever before.

Racism and Xenophobia in Virtual Russia

Stella Rock*

Introduction

Two questions are immediately begged by the title of this paper, and should be answered by way of an introduction. The first question is, why look at racism and xenophobia in 'virtual' Russia? Why not explore racism and xenophobia in the 'real' Russian Federation? The answer to this is two-fold: much valuable and detailed research and monitoring has already been done on antisemitism, xenophobia and racism within the real territory of the Russian Federation,[1]

---

* Research Fellow, Centre for German-Jewish Studies, University of Sussex.
Research for this article was supported by a Fellowship at the University of Sussex Centre for German-Jewish Studies, funded by grants from Marks & Spencer and the Conference on Jewish Material Claims Against Germany. Fieldwork in Russia was facilitated by the Open Orthodox University of Father Alexander Menn.

1. Some of the most detailed research on xenophobia and political extremism in the Russian Federation has been conducted and published by the Moscow-based NGO 'Panorama'. Many of their reports are available online at http://www.panorama.org:8100/index.html. Other monitoring agencies include the Union of Councils of Soviet Jews, Institute for Jewish Policy Research, the Anti-Defamation League Moscow.

Raphael Walden (ed.), Racism and Human Rights, *101-124.*

but precious little on the phenomenon of Russian online hate.[2] Secondly, since the mid-eighties, an increasing number of commentators have identified the Internet as a dangerous tool in the hands of fanatics, although recently some notable contributors to the debate have concluded that the medium should be viewed with less alarm than initial predications suggested.[3] Nevertheless, Governments, NGOs and international organisations remain fearful of this virtual world, and a veritable litany of reasons for this has been suggested. The Internet brings hate straight to our homes—which while providing a useful means for researchers and journalists to access extremist material, means that we feel 'invaded', exposed to propaganda we would doubtless have to work hard to find in the 'real' world. Others have perceived it as a distorting mirror—deceptively aggrandising lonely individuals or tiny splinter groups into powerful movements;[4] clothing Holocaust denial sites in pseudo-academic, respectable dress; offering a 'virtual mask' that racists can don and remove at will.[5] Some have seen in it an art form for propagandists,[6] a magical, creative, interactive medium that neo-Nazis can exploit as their predecessors exploited celluloid, or a superbly swift and flexible communication tool, a sophisticated means by which racists of the world can unite despite geographical dispersion.[7] Finally, the Internet evades all attempts at censorship, is no

2. ADL Moscow now monitors online hate and dedicated their August 2000 monthly bulletin to the subject. Western monitoring agencies have generally failed to keep abreast of developments in virtual Russia—HateWatch's former country report for Russia listed only the Pamyat website for example.

3. See for example 'HateWatch Says Goodbye...': http://www.hatewatch.org/ (last accessed May 2001). There seems to be increasing consensus amongst academics that random terrorist acts (in reality and in cyberspace) are the most likely result of Internet influence/provocation.

4. Michael Whine 'Far Right Extremists on the Internet' in *Cybercrime: Law enforcement, security and surveillance in the information age* edited by Douglas Thomas & Brian D. Loader (Routledge, London and New York 2000).

5. Les Back 'Aryans reading Adorno: Cyberculture and 21st Century Racism' forthcoming, *Journal of Ethnic and Racial Studies*.

6. See for example Anti-Defamation League Of B'nai B'rith 'Hate Group Recruitment on the Internet' (Anti-Defamation League, New York 1995): http://www.nizkor.org/hweb/orgs/american/adl/recruitment/internet-1995.html (last accessed May 2001).

7. See for example David Capitanchik and Michael Whine 'The Governance of Cyberspace: Racism on the Internet' *JPR* No. 2, July 1996 online (last accessed April 2001); Les Back 'Aryans reading Adorno'; Beverley Ray & George E. Marsh II

respecter of national boundaries or national legislation, is uncontrollable by its very size and nature.

The second question that should be answered before continuing is, why virtual Russia and not 'the global village'? Why look at the global phenomenon of racism within the confines of one nation (or more accurately, within one language group), especially when it is propagated on what is recognised as an international forum, the World Wide Web? The advantages of working within distinct language groups in a comparative way were identified during the Sussex University research project 'Racism on the Internet', which looked at English, Russian and German language material over the course of 18 months. The project identified that shared prejudices (such as the global conspiracy theory or the belief in Jewish ritual murder) were being revitalised and recreated in the global forum of the Internet, often by groups who develop and maintain international links via the Internet. However, the project also found that specific political, historical and cultural variables remain of paramount importance in influencing the presentation and propagation of prejudices, despite the global nature of the medium. As Dimitrina Petrova has observed,[8] the Soviet experience of WWII and the Holocaust accounts for significant differences between post-Soviet racism (antisemitism in particular) and Western racism. The enormous number of Soviet dead, and the suffering experienced by the population during the war, is engraved on the consciousness of those Russians who were educated during the Soviet period, partly as a result of the massive propaganda surrounding the 'Great Patriotic War'. Russian 'revisionists' have to tailor their material for an audience that is less likely than, say, an American audience, to be persuaded that Hitler was not so bad after all. They are, however, able to distort and minimize the Holocaust by relativism with ease. If over 20 million Soviet citizens died, why all the fuss about 6 million Jews? Soviet historiography also failed to educate the population about the

'Recruitment by Extremist Groups on the Internet,' in *First Monday: Peer Review Journal on the Internet* Vol. 6, No. 2 (February 2001): http://firstmonday.org/issues/issue6_2/ray/index.html (last accessed May 2001).

8. Dimitrina Petrova 'Confronting Racism in Europe: Is there a strategy in Europe?' in *Racism in Central and Eastern Europe and Beyond: Origins, Responses, Strategies. Part II, Presentations and Selected Discussions* Budapest, Hungary 19th July 2000 p. 65, available online at the website of the Office of the High Commissioner for Human Rights: http://www.unhchr.ch/huridocda/huridoca.nsf/ (last accessed May 2001).

Holocaust, leaving most Russians ignorant of the true nature of Hitler's genocidal policies.[9]

Of far more importance to Russian antisemites and extreme nationalist groups is the experience of the Bolshevik revolution, the Soviet system and the subsequent slide into chaos, which hugely influence the nature of Russian racism and xenophobia. A paper exploring the wide variety of racism on the Internet would never be able to do more than touch upon a fraction of the material—the Internet is as diverse as the humans who create it.

How Significant is Virtual Russia?

The first point that should be made is that 'virtual Russia' is not limited by national boundaries. The research conducted for this paper covered over 60 sites created by Russian citizens and hosted both abroad (mainly on US-based ISPs) and within the domain .ru, sites created by citizens of other states offering a Russian language option or with pages specially designed for the Russian viewer, and sites created by Russians living abroad. Virtual Russia in this context refers to Russian language pages.

Despite the very real obstacles to expansion of the Internet in the Russian Federation, virtual Russia is growing, geographically and demographically, at a fast rate. The biggest problem faced by providers and potential users is the inherited Soviet telecommunications system, which seriously hampers growth of networks. In 1996 only 49 per cent of urban families and 20 per cent of rural families had access to a private telephone, and this places immediate limits on the maximum number of potential users. Potential regional users (who generally survive on much lower wages than those in Moscow and Petersburg) are also excluded by the relatively high cost of Internet access in the Russian Federation,[10] and lack of access to the necessary hardware.

Despite these clear obstacles to expansion, Boston Consulting Group's Moscow office reported in March 2001 that Internet use is growing faster in Russia than anywhere else. Of Russia's 148 million inhabitants, there were 2 million users in 1999, 3 million in March 2001and a projected 7 million users

9. See Stella Rock, 'Russian Revisionism: Holocaust Denial and the New Nationalist Historiography' *Patterns of Prejudice*, vol.35, no.4, 2001.

10. Rafal Rohozinski 'How the Internet Did Not Transform Russia' *Current History* Vol. 99, No. 639 October 2000, pp.334-8.

are expected to be online in 2003. They have identified two major shifts in internet use: the first a significant growth in regional use. Currently 45 per cent of users are Moscow-based, with the remaining 55 per cent from the regions—including St Petersburg. In three years they predict that 75 per cent of users will be regional and 25 per cent Muscovites. The second major change they anticipate is a significant growth of home-based users—from 19 per cent in 1999 to 40 per cent projected for 2005. BCG believe that currently 55 per cent of users access the internet through business, and 26 per cent from government, scientific or educational institutions.[11] Other observers are even more optimistic: IDC, formerly International Data Corporation, forecasts there will be a total of 9.4 million Internet users in Russia by 2004.[12] In the year 2000 there were 45,000 webservers registered in Russia, more than three times the 1998 total (Interfax),[13] 83 Internet Service Providers (ISPs) were operating in Russia and Kazakhstan in 1999,[14] and 200 in March 2001.[15]

The other potential access point for Internet users (other than home, educational institution or work) is the Internet cafe, which has also flourished in major Russian cities. The ratings agency Expert RA reported early in 2001 that the average monthly income of Russia's leading Internet-shops gained 90 per cent during the second half of the year 2000.[16] Unfortunately there are no statistics readily available on the clientele of Internet cafes in Russia, although the director of Timeonline, the largest Moscow based Internet cafe, observes that approximately 50 per cent of his clientele are students.[17] It is probably safe to conclude that the groups with greatest access to the Internet are students, academics and white collar workers, with those in the regions who do not fall into these categories being the least likely to have access to the Internet.

---

11. *The Russia Journal* March 3-9, 2001, *The Moscow Times Business Review* May 2001 vol. 9, No. 4, p. 27
12. *The Moscow Times*, Wed January 31st 2001
13. *The Moscow Times*, Wed January 31st 2001
14. CIA World Factbook Russia 2000 report http://www.cia.gov/cia/publications/factbook/geos/rs.html (accessed March 2001)
15. *The Moscow Times Business Review* May 2001 vol. 9, No. 4, p. 27
16. *The Russia Journal* 2001-03-12 Email News Service
17. *The Moscow Times Business Review* May 2001 vol. 9, No. 4, p. 7

How Racist is Virtual Russia?

> *It seems only a matter of time before the wave of internet racism which has afflicted a number of Western European countries moves eastward with the increasing technological capabilities of post-Communist states.*[18]

For racists of all nationalities, the Internet provides an alternative to what they perceive as 'Jewish-controlled media'. Many commentators have noted the enthusiasm with which racists have embraced the new technologies, publicly welcoming the opportunities the Internet offers them to promote their cause. Recent estimates of the number of racist sites in cyberspace puts them at around 600,[19] but different monitoring agencies may well have different criteria—for example they may focus on sites that are dedicated to racist themes rather than simply containing racist material, or vice versa. Compared to the conservative figure of 600, the Simon Wiesenthal Center's 'Digital Hate 2001' CD-ROM offers to expose "more than 2,200 insidious websites that sometimes pose as high-tech fun for kids, but in fact promote hatred, anti-Semitism and terrorist violence". The racist content of a site may also vary over a period of time—sites which are not 'dedicated' to racist ideas may contain xenophobic or antisemitic material periodically, in response to public events (in the Russian context, during NATO bombing campaigns or government prosecution of the 'oligarchs' for example). An added difficulty in estimating site numbers is confusion over what constitutes a website, and the frequency with which sites move and disappear.

The only monitoring agency focusing on Russian language sites, the Anti-Defamation League (ADL) in Moscow, identified in December 2000 the existence of 64 racist websites and 3 large portals distributing racist material.[20] Only two of Simon Wiesenthal's 2,200 websites are Russian: the Pamyat website and The New Resistance.[21] A significant proportion of these sites are hosted and registered abroad. Front 14, a US portal dedicated to free hosting and email provision to 'racialists', which hosts over 300 racist sites, includes

---

18. *Racism in Central and Eastern Europe and Beyond: Origins, Responses, Strategies. Rapporteur's Notes*, Budapest, Hungary 19th July 2000 p. 20, available online at http://www.unhchr.ch/huridocda/huridoca.nsf/ (last accessed May 2001).
19. See for example Les Back 'Aryans reading Adorno'.
20. *Anti-Semitism in Russia 2000* (ADL Moscow Report).
21. Rick Eaton (SWC Research), e-mail correspondence 10th May 2001.

at least eight Russian language sites amongst its clientele. Rus-sky,[22] a major Russian Orthodox site which carries antisemitic and revisionist material, is registered to a Russian living in South Dakota, USA.

The popularity of these sites is also open to question. Site rating engines cannot distinguish between academics, researchers or monitoring agencies, and dedicated racists or sympathetic surfers for example, although they do allow one to make basic assumptions about which sites are most 'visible'. Results gleaned from the sites of Top.list[23] and Rambler suggest that the better known an organisation or publication is in the 'real world', the more visible it is in cyberspace. The popular nationalist newspaper *Zavtra*, for example, which frequently propagates antisemitic material, ranked in first place on Top.list in the category Russian Government>Politics on May 8th 2001, with over 7,000 visitors.

The ADL's recent report *Poisoning the Web: Hatred Online. Internet Bigotry, Extremism and Violence* suggests that

> While deeply disturbing, the growth of hate and extremism on the Internet simply mirrors the expansion of Internet use. What began as a small computer network used primarily by scientists and academic researchers has become a mass medium. Over 147 million people worldwide now use the Internet, 79 million of whom are in the United States.

As Internet use expands in the Russian Federation, we should expect the number of racist and xenophobic sites to increase. One could also add that the extent of hate and extremism on the Internet mirrors the extent of hate and extremism in society, although as previously observed, the Internet can act as a distorting mirror which portrays numerically insignificant groups as professional organisations. In the Russian case, I suggest that while individual sites may inaccurately reflect the strength and organisational capabilities of marginal groups, the volume of xenophobic and antisemitic material is not at odds with the current climate in the Russian Federation.[24] If anything, it is less

22. http://www.rus-sky.com (last accessed May 2001)
23. http://top.list.ru (last accessed May 2001)
24. See for example the IJPR report on *Antisemitism and Xenophobia in the Russian Federation* at http://www.axt.org.uk/antisem/countries/russia/index.html to which the author contributed, and *Vek* No. 17, April 2001 on the increasing popularity of extreme right-wing groups amongst young Russians.

than might be expected, as political parties whose members include notable antisemites and extreme nationalists (The Communist Party of the Russian Federation, the inaptly-named Liberal Democratic Party of Russia) tend to maintain relatively 'clean' websites.

The Territory

Most of the websites that I surveyed during the course of my research are the creations of marginal nationalist parties and movements, and of religious organisations. A significant number of racist and antisemitic newspapers and journals are also available online, some (such as the National-Socialist *Shturmovik*) after having been closed down in print, but most easily available in hard copy at least in Moscow. It is not possible in this paper (and would be repetitive and unenlightening) to map the terrain in detail, and I have left the issue of Usenet newsgroups aside altogether as they require a different type of research, and are already being abandoned for different technologies by dedicated racists in the West. What follows is a survey of some of the more significant websites in virtual Russia, from which I draw general conclusions.

Michael Whine has already observed that one function of the Internet is the establishment of common networks around a shared enemy,[25] despite significant ideological differences. The primary shared enemy in virtual Russia (as in the global community of racists) is the Jew, with NATO, the USA (sometimes simply 'the West') and non-Slavic ethnic minorities—Chechens or people from the Caucuses, blacks and Asians as runners-up in the hate parade. This use of xenophobia and racism to bind disparate individuals and groups together is not exclusive to the Internet, nor is it a new phenomenon. It was intrinsic to the behaviour of various groups in the Russian Empire of the late nineteenth and early twentieth centuries,[26] who found in antisemitism (as do their modern-day counterparts) a unifying programme for those whose politi-

---

25. Michael Whine 'Cyberspace: A New Medium for Communication, Command and Control by Extremists' April 1999. Available online at http://www.ict.org.il/articles/cyberspace.htm (last accessed April 2001).

26. See for example Andras Kovacs 'Xenophobia, Anti-Semitism and the Extreme Right in Europe' in *Racism in Central and Eastern Europe and Beyond: Origins, Responses, Strategies. Part II Presentations and Selected Discussions* p. 55, available online at http://www.unhchr.ch/huridocda/huridoca.nsf/

cal ideology is thin, illogical or non-existent. Antisemitism is common to virtual (and real) communities of skinheads, neo-pagans, Orthodox Christians, monarchists, neo-Nazis, National-Bolsheviks and Eurasianists. 'Scapegoating' Jews for the failings of post-Soviet society and for the brutalities of the Soviet regime, for the collapse of the Soviet Union or the Russian Empire, for the murder of the Tsar and destruction of a 'golden' past, provides these diverse groups with an easy explanation for Russia's sorrows.

This politically diverse, racist community uses the Internet primarily for propaganda. This propaganda can serve a three-fold purpose: to recruit new members or attract sympathisers, to educate/indoctrinate the sympathetic, and to publicise the organisation. Notwithstanding the intention, there is little evidence to suggest that Internet propaganda is effective as a means of recruitment.[27] In Russia, where the most ready audience for extremist propaganda—the impoverished residents of the provinces, urban youth with low level education and bitter resentment for the New Russia—has almost no access to the Internet, it seems even less likely that the websites play a significant role in attracting new members. Some observers of Russian National Unity (RNE), which until the split in September 1999 was the most successful of the neo-Nazi groups (membership figures have been estimated at between 7,000 and 15,000, with a much larger support base of sympathisers) have identified RNE's appeal to 'deprived and neglected youth' as initially a material and psychological one (the prospect of free uniforms, sports, military training, of 'belonging' to a strong group), with ideological indoctrination following recruitment.[28]

Internet propaganda which is not necessarily primarily directed at recruitment is viewed by some observers as a PR exercise, aimed at journalists and researchers. Slava Likhachev of the Moscow-based Panorama agency, which monitors racism, xenophobia and political extremism in the Russian Federation, comments that the Russian National Unity website as it existed before the split was written mostly by journalists (much of the information on the site being taken directly from newspaper articles) for journalists. An organisation needs to have a visible web presence 'to be taken seriously',[29]

---

27. David Capitanchik and Michael Whine 'The Governance of Cyberspace: Racism on the Internet' *JPR* No. 2, July 1996.

28. See Stephen Shenfield *Russian Fascism: Traditions, Tendencies, Movements* (M.E. Sharpe, New York 2001) pp. 132-136.

29. Interview with Slava Likhachev (Panorama, Moscow), September 2000.

that is, to be discussed in mainstream media. The fragmented nature of the extreme nationalist movement is evidenced by the competing websites—RNE now has three websites each proclaiming their own version of the organisation's 'truth'.[30] Despite the potentially unifying nature of the Internet, fragmentation and fratricidal competition for members and political significance remain a problem for Russian extremist groups.

One example of an umbrella site (established in May 2000) which attempts to provide a unifying forum for nationalists of various colours (some racist to an extreme degree) is nationalism.org, 'Norg'. At the time of writing (May 2001), Norg rates on Top.list in the category Russian Government>Politics at number four (101 on Rambler's 'Top 100'), in comparison to *Zavtra*, the extremist newspaper which comes in at number 1, Dugin's antisemitic site Arctogeia which is number 2 on Top.list and 55 on Rambler, the liberal political party Yabloko (number 3) and Russian Skinheads at number 5 on Top.list. Norg hosts 16 sites, several of which are personal pages expounding the authors' views on various topics, but most of which are organisational.

Norg manages to unify in cyberspace religious fundamentalists, neo-Nazis, would-be philosophers, pro-Serbian activists, anti-Eurasianists, and pan-Slavicists. Kasimovsky's revamped movement Russian Action[31] (he formerly led the Russian National-Socialist Party) and the Brotherhood of St Joseph Volotsky—which states its 'active collaboration' with Kasimovsky's movement—are two of the most xenophobic sites, after Russian Skins, which in honour of Hitler's birthday carries a series of pictures showing the Führer with suitably Aryan babies. One cannot conclude from this unity in cyberspace that any mutual, organisational support (other than advertising each other's propaganda) exists however, despite online declarations. The collaboration between Kasimovsky's organisation and the Brotherhood of St Joseph Volotsky (who declare their main aims to be the unification of the Russian Orthodox Church and the education of the intelligentsia[32]) apparently consists of a per-

30. http://www.barkashov-rne.nm.ru/ 'Barkashov's Guards' (last accessed May 2001).
http://www.rne.org/vopd/index3.shtml (last accessed May 2001).
http://www.rne.faithweb.com/ 'Russian Revival' (last accessed May 2001).

31. Kasimovsky's website http://nationalism.org/rusaction/ (last accessed May 2001) shows the tendency in evidence within the national-patriot movement towards 'respectability'—created in the 'David Duke' style rather than the 'Russian Skins' style of his old RNSP pages.

32. Interview with Andrei Zhukov, Brotherhood of St Joseph Volotsky, Moscow 30th April 2001.

sonal relationship between Anatoli Makeev, the 'elder' of the brotherhood, and Kasimovsky, and Makeev's membership on the editorial board of Kasimovsky's newspaper *Right Resistance*.[33]

Joint public actions do occur however—a march planned for Victory Day (May 9th) which united 'national-patriotic' organisations was advertised on the web pages of the Union of Orthodox Banner Bearers, advising would-be participants when and where to meet, and what to bring with them (icons, flags etc.). Potential attendees were advised that the group would be carrying a banner declaring 'Freedom for Colonel Budanov', a Russian army officer who allegedly raped and strangled an eighteen year old Chechen girl.[34] A similar 'krestnyi khod' (an Orthodox march with icons) advertised on the same website for the 19th May was attended by members of Pamyat, the Black Hundreds, the People's Nationalist Party and the Union of Orthodox Banner Bearers. It is not clear that Internet advertising significantly influences the numbers attending such events however.

A second problem faced by any organisation which has aspirations to be Russia-wide (and any party hoping to enter candidates in elections must, according to the Federal Law on public associations, be a federal-wide political association with branches in a minimum of 45 regions or provinces[35]) is geographical distance. Again, using Barkashov's RNE website[36] as an example, it would appear that the Internet has proved a useful tool in maintaining links between regional branches. Contact details and times of meetings for the numerous regional branches are available, plus news of various events, and in the case of unruly regions the expulsion 'orders' of Barkashov appear when that region's button is clicked on. Despite this, one of the apparent reasons for the split was Moscow's inability to control the strong regional bases,[37] so information technology has had limited success in this area too.

---

33. Interview with Anatoli Mikhailovich Makeev, Brotherhood of St Joseph Volotsky, Moscow 30th April 2001. This may be a disingenuous reply to a question posed by a Western researcher, but as yet I have found no evidence of organisational collaborative activity.
34. http://www.rus-sky.com/horugvenosec/info/090501.htm (last accessed May 2001).
35. The European Union's Project for Capacity Development in Election Monitoring, *Briefing Document 13: Spas Profile*, 08/12/99.
36. http://www.barkashov-rne.nm.ru/ (Barkashov's Guards).
37. Interview with Slava Likhachev (Panorama, Moscow), September 2000.

In addition to bringing dispersed members together in cyberspace, the Internet has been helpful in forging at least virtual collaboration between Russian nationalists and their like-minded brethren abroad. Most extremist sites offer an English language, and sometimes a German language option, and host links to other racist and extremist organisations abroad. Lev Krichevsky, director of the Moscow office of the Anti-Defamation League, claims that extreme Russian nationalists are stepping up contacts with their counterparts in the West, including the sharing of Internet resources. 'It is amazing to see how fast these guys, with all their anti-Western rhetoric, find common language and organize multi-language Web sites together with their colleagues from the West'.[38] This remark was prompted by the visit to Moscow of the most prominent Western racist to make the transition from virtual Russia to real Russia, David Duke, whose involvement with Russian extremists is well documented. Duke, who appears to have visited Russia three times in two years, refers to Moscow as 'the Whitest' of Europe's capital cities in a Summer 2000 article entitled 'Is Russia the Key to White Survival?'. Duke writes that

> The Russian people also have a much greater knowledge of the power of International Zionism and the dominant Jewish role in orchestrating the immigration and multiculturalism that is undermining the West... I think Russia is so important to the worldwide efforts for our people that the new book will actually have its first printing in Russia a few weeks before the English edition will appear... We cannot win this struggle unless we stand indivisible against an implacable enemy whose hatred for us has grown and deepened for two millennia.[39]

A Yandex 'link to' search[40] shows that Duke's site is linked to by Rus-sky and a Ukrainian skinhead site, and Duke's visit was covered by various nationalist websites, including Kasimovsky's Russian Action. It is also available on the English language pages of one of the three RNE websites.[41]

While many of the websites of racist organisations appear to use the Internet to organise and influence real world activities—carrying notices of forthcoming events, encouraging surfers to vote for particular candidates etc.—limited

---

38. Lev Gorodetsky "Duke's message to Russians: Anti-Semites of the world, unite" *JTA* 4th September 2000: http://www.jta.org/story.asp?story=6184.

39. http://www.duke.org/dukereport/10-00.html (last accessed February 2001).

40. Yandex—http://www.yandex.ru—is one of the most popular Russian search engines. A 'link to' search identifies sites which link to the URL specified.

41. http://www.rne.org/vopd/english/duke.html.

use is, as yet, made of the interactive potential of the medium. Technical proficiency is increasing however. For example, the old People's Socialist Worker's Party site[42] ran a primitive, propaganda-driven online survey from October to December 1999 which asked: 'Who, in your opinion governs the country?' Respondents were invited to choose between 'An invalid' (a reference to Yeltsin's failing health, which allegedly attracted a 5 per cent response), 'The ethnic oligarchy' (aka the Jewish oligarchy—44 per cent), 'CIA and MOSSAD' (34 per cent), Patriots of Russia (4 per cent), or to simply respond 'I spit on this country!', which 13 per cent of respondents chose to do. This can hardly have provided helpful information for the Party organisers. In May 2001 however, the redesigned website offered a more complex survey which allowed respondents more than one choice in answer to the question 'Who would you like to see in an All-Russia union of patriots?' (the options given are 'Nationalists', 'Monarchists', 'Communists', 'Orthodox', 'Pagans', 'Other religious confessions', 'Liberal-Democrat patriots').[43] This at least indicates some desire to use information gained via the Internet for strategic planning. This website also now offers an e-mail news service to subscribers, and a discussion board.

A few sites directly advocate acts of violence, or offer lessons on warfare techniques. A personal website[44]—which offers a detailed list of Russian nationalist groups, including manifestos, membership statistics and web addresses for the undecided—includes a list of prominent Russian Jews (with names, addresses, and telephone numbers) identified as partly responsible for the 'genocide' against the Russian people,[45] with the suggestion that the surfer find and punish these offenders. Project Rodina ('Homeland'), which maintains the appearance of a respectable online journal with articles by Dostoevsky ('On the Jewish Question', naturally) for example, offers a 'tactics of partisan warfare' section under the heading 'To Arms' which insists that:

> Materials, published in this section, are not a call to some sort of illegal action, nor the propaganda of violence. Simply we consider that this information may prepare any person for the defence of the Homeland.[46]

---

42. http://www.chat.ru/~nsrp/ (last accessed December 2000).
43. http://nsrp.nm.ru/ (last accessed May 2001).
44. http://front14.org/russian/ (last accessed May 2001). This site has now been reported to the FSB, via ADL Moscow.
45. http://www.front14.org/russian/spisok.htm (last accessed December 2000).
46. http://nationalism.org/rodina/ (last accessed May 2001); my translation.

Several of the most extremist sites[47] offer photographs of their members 'in training'—firing guns, dressed in combat gear—photos which are clearly designed to impress potential recruits and intimidate 'enemies'. One of the most visually intimidating sites belongs to the antisemitic neo-pagan Church of Nav, which portrays its members in white robes with pointed black hoods, in Ku Klux Klan style.[48]

Perhaps the most startling racist community in virtual Russia is that of the Russian Orthodox. Their significant—even disproportionate—presence mirrors a depressing post-Soviet reality. The search for national identity that attended the collapse of the Soviet Union and the attendant State-sponsored ideology of proletarian internationalism and 'the Soviet citizen' (however hypocritical and flawed) has attracted to the Russian Orthodox Church a great number of individuals whose 'spirituality' rests in ethnic pride and resentment of Western (often synonymous with 'Jewish') civilization. Many of the most extreme nationalists gravitate toward the Russian Orthodox Church Abroad, the True Orthodox Church (also known as the Catacomb Church) and Old Belief, viewing the Moscow Patriarchate as somehow contaminated by its prior collaboration with the 'satanic' Communist regime and public fraternisation with Jews and other infidels. This view of the Church is not exclusive to those who reject the Moscow Patriarchate though. Leonid Simonov, head of the Union of Orthodox Brotherhoods and of the Union of Orthodox Banner Bearers, declares online that:

> Really, it has long ceased to be a secret that in our contemporary Church there is as it were two parallel churches—the church of Hellenes, that is the Russians, and the Church of the Jews...
>
> ...The prophet monk Avel said, that on Rus there were [imposed] two yokes—the Tartar-Mongol and the Polish-Lithuanian, and there will be one more—the most terrible—the YIDDISH. And we, brothers and sisters, are suffering it now with you. But one should never remain indifferent, one must never sleep, never simply pray—one must fight, brothers and sisters, we need to fight for the freeing of our homeland from the yiddish yoke![49]

---

47. See Pamyat's http://www.geocities.com/Colosseum/Loge/8461/phototek.html for example (last accessed May 2001).

48. http://i.am/navi1/ (last accessed May 2001).

49. http://www.rus-sky.com/horugvenosec/simonovich/heresy.htm (last accessed April 2001); my translation.

Those who remain within the Moscow Patriarchate wield disproportionate influence through their successful exploitation of mass media—both liberals and Orthodox patriots recognise that the weakness of official Church publications and the massive output of the fundamentalist nationalists are the key to their success.[50] Online, the nature of the message (which is often extremely antisemitic, propagating the myth of Jewish ritual murder and the infamous *Protocols of the Elders of Zion* for example) is 'legitimised' by the Orthodox 'dressing' given it by the website creators. Rus-sky,[51] a deceptively respectable-looking website which hosts the above cited web pages of the Union of Orthodox Banner Bearers, also archives articles such as 'About Jewish Fascism' by Boris Mironov, a former Minister of the Press under Yeltsin.[52] In this article, Mironov states that:

> The myth of antisemitism—the persecution and oppression of Jews in Russia, like the myth of the holocaust—the destruction by the Germans of six million Jews—is fantastical, lucrative Jewish trickery, built up lovingly by the yids in masterly fashion, from which, out of nothing, out of mere noise, by the wagging of tongues, colossal amounts of money are created.[53]

This large virtual community maintains links with the Russian émigré community in America, and it is probable that their successful presence on the Internet is supported financially and technically by their American-based brethren. That said, the Russia-based Russkaia Linia,[54] an 'Orthodox Information Agency' with close links to the antisemitic 'disciples' of the late Metropolitan Ioann of St Petersburg, is as technologically proficient and prolific as its American-based rival.

---

50. Interviews with Sergei Chapnin, a journalist from the liberal-leaning online magazine *Sobornost* (Moscow, 18th January 2001) and Anatoli Stepanov, editor of the extreme nationalist *Russian Orthodox Patriot* and political editor of the online Orthodox Information Agency 'Russkaia Linia' (St. Petersburg, 20th February 2001).
51. http://www.rus-sky.com
52. See http://www.vii.org/monroe/issue09/portrait.htm (last accessed February 2001).
53. Boris Mironov'About Jewish Fascism' first published in *Kolokol* Nos. 107 & 108 dated 5th & 12th June 1998; available online at http://www.rus-sky.org/history/library/articles/mironov1.htm (last accessed October 2000).
54. http://www.rusk.ru/

What Is to Be Done?

Recommendation 24: 'Governments should monitor the abuse of technology, especially the Internet, as a vector for hate speech and incitement to hate crime and violence. They should involve the Internet community in seeking judicial, technical and moral measures.'[55]

Judicial measures

It has been suggested that 'the Internet should not be regarded differently from other means of publishing and disseminating speech and ideas. The same laws and controls which already apply to other means of publishing, whether electronic or printed, should be applied to the Internet.'[56]

The Russian Federation's current Constitution and Criminal Code would appear to provide adequate grounds to prosecute those propagating racism and antisemitism by any means:

> Article 13, par. 5 of the RF Constitution prohibits creation and activities of the public associations, whose aims and actions are targeted... at 'exciting social, racial, national and religious hostility'; Article 29 which proclaims freedom of thought and speech, also contains a prohibition on 'propaganda or agitation inciting social, racial, national or religious hatred and enmity'[57]

Article No. 282 of the Criminal Code clearly defines the offence of arousing national, racial or religious hatred, and the appropriate sentence for perpetrators. It states:

1. Efforts to arouse national, racial or religious hatred, to demean national worth, or to propagate the exclusivity, superiority or inferiority of citizens on the basis of their attitude to religion, nationality or race shall, if

55. *UN Report of the Central and Eastern European regional seminar of experts on the protection of minorities and other vulnerable groups and strengthening human rights capacity at the national level (Warsaw, 5-7 July 2000)* available online at http://www.unhchr.ch/huridocda/huridoca.nsf/

56. David Capitanchik and Michael Whine 'The Governance of Cyberspace: Racism on the Internet'.

57. *Compliance of the Russian Federation with the Convention on the Elimination of All Forms of Racial Discrimination* Report By The Memorial Human Rights Centre, Moscow, November 2000 (addressed to the World Conference Against Racism, Racial Discrimination, Xenophobia and Related Intolerance); available online: http://www.memo.ru/hr/discrim/ethnic/disce00.htm (last accessed May 2001).

committed in public or through the mass media, be punishable by a fine of between 500 and 800 times the minimum wage, or of the wages or other income of the perpetrator for a period of between five and eight months, or by restrictions on the perpetrator's freedom for a period of up to three years, or by imprisonment of between two and four years.

2. The same offence, when:
   a. accompanied by violence or the threat of violence,
   b. committed by an individual taking advantage of his official position, or
   c. committed by an organized group

   shall be punishable by imprisonment of between three and five years.[58]

The Law 'On Mass Media', Article 4, also prohibits 'the abuse of freedom of speech' which covers the propagation of violence and incitement of racial hatred. Despite the various legislative options available, it is widely acknowledged that the judicial system and the law-enforcement bodies are unable or unwilling to adequately address the issue.[59] Vast amounts of defamatory and inflammatory xenophobic material are available in print and online, and antisemitism has been propagated even in the mainstream media.[60] Antisemitic public statements by politicians have also failed to draw censure from the Duma. In a speech to rallies in Moscow in October 1998 (later shown repeatedly on television) for example, General Makashov of the Communist Party of the Russian Federation announced 'I will round up all the Yids and send them to the next world!' A Duma motion censuring him for his 'harsh, abusive statements' and for inciting racial hatred was defeated by 121 votes to 107.[61] It

---

58. UN Committee On The Elimination Of Racial Discrimination *Reports Submitted By States Parties Under Article 9 Of The Convention: Fourteenth periodic reports of States parties due in 1994, Addendum, Russian Federation* (CERD/C/299/Add.15) 28 July 1998; available online: http://www.hri.ca/fortherecord1998/documentation/tbodies/cerd-c-299-add15.htm (last accessed May 2001).

59. See the Memorial 2000 report to the World Conference, the conclusions of which are supported by other NGOs including ADL Moscow.

60. A recent example which appeared in *Nezavisimaya Gazeta* 7th September 2000 is an article by the General Director of the Information Analytical Agency of the Department of Affairs, part of the Presidential Administration, about the global Jewish-Masonic plot to control world government.

61. http://www.axt.org.uk/antisem/countries/russia/index.html

is hardly surprising that 'there has been no indication...that law enforcement forces tend to take hate-related Web activities with due seriousness.'[62]

The government of the Russian Federation is already well placed to monitor the spread of racist propaganda on the Internet should it choose to do so, since Russian ISPs are required by law to link their computers to the FSB, the successor to the KGB. Under an amendment signed into law by Putin and taking effect from January 2000, an additional seven law-enforcement bodies have been authorised to monitor e-mail and other electronic traffic.[63] It is further proposed that all Internet publications will need to register with the Communications Ministry if they want to be considered members of the mass media, a status which gives both tax breaks and official recognition.[64] However, in finding solutions to the problem of racism in post-Soviet Eastern Europe the importance of protecting free speech in fragile democracies should be addressed,[65] and it is clear that this is not high on the current government's agenda. It is also clear that one can overstate the concern of Russian citizens to preserve their new freedoms. A nationwide poll conducted by VCIOM in October 2000 found that 36 per cent of respondents would certainly or probably support the temporary limiting of freedom of speech and democratic elections, 52 per cent probably or certainly would be against such a limitation, and 12 per cent could not answer the question. 55 per cent of respondents also stated that they expected and hoped that Putin would strengthen state control over the media.[66]

Disregarding arguments about whether the state should proactively pursue 'hate speech' and the legitimacy of their tactics, currently national legislation can be easily bypassed by racists, who simply move their offending websites to

62. Anti-Semitism in Russia 2000 (ADL Moscow Report).

63. See CPJ briefing paper: http://www.cpj.org/Briefings/Russia_analysis_Marchoo/Russia_analysis_marchoo.html and also Leonard R. Sussman's 'The Internet and Press Freedom 2000', available online at: http://freedomhouse.org/pfs2000/sussman.html (last accessed March 2001).

64. *The Moscow Times* January 31st 2001.

65. Nils Muiznieks 'The Struggle against Racism and Xenophobia in Central and Eastern Europe: Trends, Obstacles and Prospects' (HR/WSW/SEM.2/2000/BP.1) presented as part of the *UN Report of the Central and Eastern European regional seminar of experts on the protection of minorities and other vulnerable groups and strengthening human rights capacity at the national level (Warsaw, 5-7 July 2000)*; available online at http://www.unhchr.ch/huridocda/huridoca.nsf/

66. http://www.russiavotes.org/ (last accessed May 2001).

US-based servers. America's prioritising of the right to free speech has created a haven for racists of all nationalities, and as we have seen, a significant number of Russian racists have taken refuge there—ironically, given the anti-US feelings harboured by many of them. As Michael Whine points out,

> Any international action that is considered must now inevitably focus on the fact that much offensive and illegal material originates in America, where the First Amendment to the Constitution protects all free expression of opinion except that which directly incites violence.[67]

Technical Measures

Recently ADL Moscow have achieved some measure of success working with ISPs to stem the flow of racist propaganda online.

> ADL contacted access providers urging them to adopt policies that would stop dissemination of hateful materials by some of their clients. Resulting from those contacts, a number of Web-sites containing anti-Semitism had been closed down.[68]

They further suggest that such positive action would have greater effect if ISPs, instead of simply deleting the site, would replace it with a notice stating that the offending pages have been removed because 'antisemitism and fascism are dangerous'.[69] Unfortunately, we have witnessed the development of services by racists to overcome the lobbying of activists like the ADL. Front14, who host websites written around the world, declare:

> Many White people don't have the time and energy to put into hosting their own domain, so they join Geocities, Angelfire, etc, in an attempt to get their voices heard. But these 'free' services (who bombard you with ads) have adopted an aggressive anti-White policy. We decided to provide an alternative to proud White men and women, one that would be for our White interests only.... When you sign up for a Front 14 account, you will receive 10 MB of webspace, and POP/Web-based Email. We also

67. *International Co-operation to Combat the Use of the Internet for the Purposes of Incitement to Racial Hatred* Report sent to Mary Robinson at the UNHCR Geneva, on 2 August 1999 by the Board of Deputies of British Jews. Courtesy of Michael Whine.
68. Anti-Semitism In Russia 2000 (ADL Moscow Report).
69. ADL *Antisemitism and Xenophobia in the Russian Federation Bulletin* No. 5 August 2000; my translation.

> offer our users counters, guestbooks, message boards, polls, and free advertising on the Front 14 website.[70]

David Sitman, Head of Computer Communications and Databases at the Louis Calder, Jr. Computation Center based at Tel Aviv University suggests a solution that may impact significantly on the visibility of racist sites thereby reducing any influence their propaganda may hold for the uninitiated:

> While it is true that the Internet, unlike radio and television, allows global access, and in that sense the potential audience for any site is now more than 100 million, if a site cannot be found, it will not get visitors. Today's leading web indexing sites (such as Yahoo!) and search engine sites (such as AltaVista, Lycos and Infoseek) cover only a small portion of all the pages in the global Internet. As these sites redefine themselves as Internet 'portals'—full-service entry points for all Internet usage, access to Internet resources is being centralized in the hands of a small number of key players controlled by large commercial interests. Sites which are unknown or unacceptable to the new Internet information oligarchy will be marginalized.[71]

ADL Moscow agrees that the key to marginalising racist sites lies with search engines:

> Undoubtedly, if the owners of search engines did not include similar sites in the ratings (such as Yandex, Rambler and Aport in the .ru zone), access to them would be complicated many times over.[72]

These suggested solutions rely heavily on the co-operation of ISPs and commercial companies, but still offer more potential success than the partial solutions of blocking and filtering software, the limitations of which are well-documented.

Positive Counteraction and Conclusions

I have chosen 'positive counteraction' as a sub-heading in place of 'moral measures', as it better describes what I would suggest is the best way to address

70. http://front14.org/indexold.htm (last accessed May 2001).
71. David Sitman 'Hate On The Internet: A Cause For Concern?' Anti-Semitism Worldwide 1998/9 (Stephen Roth website) http://www.tau.ac.il:81/Anti-Semitism/asw98-9/sitman.html
72. ADL *Antisemitism and Xenophobia in the Russian Federation Bulletin* No. 5 August 2000; my translation.

the issues raised by this paper. There seem to me to be two key points which help to explain the current growth of Internet racism in virtual Russia, and which to a great extent explain the failure of the current system to curb it. Both these issues, I would argue, need to be tackled in a positive (rather than a 'punitive') fashion.

1. The last decade has created a society in which economic and social inequalities are glaring and ubiquitous, and for which the population was psychologically unprepared. The sharp population decrease as a result of alcohol and drug abuse, poverty-related diseases, stress and depression, coupled with inadequate medical and social services, is cited as evidence of what some racists are now calling the 'genocide of the Russian nation'. Racists exploit the jealousy, bitterness and loss of self-worth experienced by the numerous losers which 'wild' capitalism created in post-Soviet Russia. The collapse of the former Soviet empire, the resulting chaos, ethnic tension and the perceived 'humiliation' of Russia have also created a ready audience of patriots old and young who long to find an 'alien' (or perhaps more accurately a non-Slavic) enemy to blame.
2. Racism, xenophobia and antisemitism are neither confined to the margins of society nor to any particular strata of the population. They can be found amongst intellectuals,[73] the working class, mainstream politics, the army, the Church—in all spheres of Russian life. Those few politicians who have consistently spoken out against racism have fared badly; Grigory Yavlinsky of the liberal Yabloko party won a miserable 5.8 per cent of the vote in the recent presidential elections. It is difficult for those in positions of authority (whether in the government or in institutions such as the Russian Orthodox Church) to take a moral stance on the racist activities of extremist groups, when their own houses are so clearly in disorder.

To counter-balance these depressing observations, it should be noted that the last decade has seen a strong NGO human rights movement emerge, with an active programme of monitoring, lobbying and education work. Any measures to address the issue of racism on the Internet must be developed and imple-

73. See for example Vadim Rossman 'The Ethnic Community and its Enemies: Russian Intellectual Antisemitism in the Post-Communist Era' in the SICSA Annual Report, October 2000.

mented with the full participation of those who are already working to change the current climate of intolerance.

The current administration has made an attempt to deal with the issue of racism by the creation of the Federal 'Interdepartmental Programme for the Creation of Tolerance and the Prevention of Extremism in Civil Society', the main aim of which is the development and realisation of an effective State policy to that end.[74] This programme is as yet in its infancy, and so has had little impact, although it is already working with the Holocaust Centre in Moscow to develop education programmes that will go some way to counteracting antisemitic 'revisionist' propaganda in circulation, and the ignorance of Hitler's genocidal policies which is the legacy of the Soviet education system.[75] The programme, which unites federal departments and academics from Moscow State University, is also providing 'tolerance' training for police, social workers and medical staff providing services to ethnic minorities and refugees, and there are plans to publish research on racism and extremism on the Internet this year.[76]

Education programmes aiming to counteract racist propaganda must make use of the media exploited by the racists, and as observed, the strength of extreme nationalists within the Church for example is built on their successful exploitation of mass media, including the Internet. The positive potential of the Internet has already been identified by the Office of the High Commissioner for Human Rights:

> The Internet can ... also serve as a tool in the fight against racism, racial discrimination, xenophobia and related intolerance. The use of the Internet to distribute positive information and materials, research and facts about immigrants and minorities can support action against racism and anti-Semitism, raise awareness, promote understanding and increase tolerance.[77]

---

74. The Centre for Social Innovation website: http://www.innovations.ru/tolerant/ (last accessed May 2001).

75. Interview with Dr Ilya Altman, Holocaust Centre, Moscow, 9th April 2001.

76. Interview with Professor Alexander G. Asmolov, Moscow State University, author of the Federal Programme and one of the Programme initiators, and Galina Soldatova, Moscow, 15th April 2001.

77. Office of the High Commissioner for Human Rights (OHCHR) *Consultation on the use of the Internet for the purpose of incitement to racial hatred, racial propaganda and xenophobia* (A/CONF.189/PC.1/5) 5th April 2000; available on the United Nations website: http://www.unhchr.ch/

In attempting to address these issues, we should be aware of the fact that educational institutions provide one of the main access points for Internet users in the Russian Federation. The Internet offers an ideal medium for reaching not just one generation but several—the current generation of students will form the next generation of school teachers and university lecturers, and now is the time to develop materials to be disseminated on rapidly expanding provincial networks.

Finally, given the prominence of the Russian Orthodox Church in the formation of post-Soviet national identity and its unhappy (although arguably unintentional) role in the propagation of antisemitism, I would argue that it is essential to involve Orthodox leaders, in conjunction with religious leaders of other religions of the multi-ethnic Russian Federation, in the development of measures to combat xenophobia and intolerance. There is some movement on the part of the Church in this direction already. In November 2000 Metropolitan Kiril attended the Interreligious Peace Forum in Moscow, at which spiritual leaders of Christianity, Islam, Buddhism and Judaism issued a statement declaring 'We are seriously disturbed by acts of vandalism to sacred places, manifestations of xenophobia and sacrilege, propaganda of prejudicial attitudes toward religion and public actions that offend the feelings of believers.'[78]

The Patriarch too has seen the potential benefits of the Internet, and blessed all users of the official Church website, saying:

> The use of new opportunities of the global computer communications gives another example of this position [the openness of the Church]. Now the news of current events in the life of the Russian Orthodox Church and of various aspects of her ministry could be received undistorted through our official server in the Internet. I hope that it would indeed serve to the good cause of reconciliation and would help understand the ministry of the Church in the world more profoundly.[79]

It would indeed serve the good cause of reconciliation if the Orthodox surfer were able to distinguish easily between those websites which are sanctioned by the Patriarch, and those which (one hopes) would be identified by the Patriarchate as inimical to the true spirit of Russian Orthodoxy, and if the official webserver could host material promoting tolerance to counter-balance the aggressive xenophobia of some Orthodox in cyberspace.

---

78. http://www.axt.org.uk/antisem/countries/russia/index.html.
79. http://www.russian-orthodox-church.org.ru/pa2_gr_en.htm (last accessed December 2000).

In conclusion, I would suggest that we should be afraid of our virtual Russia not because it exists in a dangerous medium that has the power to corrupt, or distort, or strengthen neo-Nazi networks, or even incite violence. While all of these may be to varying degrees true, I would argue that the most disturbing aspect of virtual Russia is that it reflects a real nation where the spirit of intolerance and xenophobia has affected all strata of society.

In addressing the problem of racism in virtual Russia, I would argue that positive counter-measures (particularly in the sphere of education) are likely to yield the best results, as judicial measures are currently ineffectual and likely to remain so in the prevailing climate of antisemitism and xenophobia. Similarly, it seems likely that racists will continue to grow in technological proficiency, and find creative solutions to any technical solution that might be imposed to limit their Internet activity. Finally, I would argue that because of the pervasive nature of racism in Russian society, special measures directed against racism on the Internet are likely to prove ineffectual unless more comprehensive and general work is initiated to address the issues that racists are exploiting so successfully: poverty, personal insecurity, inequality, the desire to find a scapegoat rather than acknowledge past mistakes, the need to create a national identity, to feel both individual self-worth and national pride.

Unease in the Global Village: German-language Racism on the Internet

Rebekah Webb*

Introduction

According to the European Union Monitoring Centre on Racism and Xenophobia (EUMC), Internet technology has given racist and extremist movements previously in decline 'a new lease of life'.[1] According to their most recent Annual Report, the number of websites registered in Germany calling for racist and xenophobic violence more than doubled in the year 2000 from 330 to 800.[2] Germany is one of only two countries in the EU to have

---

* Research Associate, Centre for German-Jewish Studies, University of Sussex. Research for this article was undertaken as part of the Racism on the Internet project funded by grants from Marks & Spencer and the Conference of Material Claims Against Germany.

1. *Diversity and Equality for Europe: Annual Report 1999* (European Monitoring Centre on Racism and Xenophobia, Vienna), p. 47.
2. *Diversity and Equality for Europe, Annual Report 2000* (European Monitoring Centre on Racism and Xenophobia, Vienna), p. 24.

Raphael Walden (ed.), Racism and Human Rights, *125-141.*

shown an increase in the number of propaganda crimes with racist content in the year 2000.[3] The Stephen Roth Institute, one of the many centres monitoring racism on the Internet, has also reported large increases in the number of German-language racist sites over the past two years, finding that up to one in five contains material which violates German law.[4] These figures roughly correspond with those from the German Federal Office for the Protection of the Constitution (*Bundesamt für Verfassungsschutz*), which last year had knowledge of at least 800 German-based extremist right-wing home pages: 'the Internet has become a vehicle for aggressive propaganda'.[5]

German-language racism is an interesting case study within the context of Internet racism in general for a number of reasons. Firstly, Internet racism in any language often draws on National Socialist ideas. Not all extremists are neo-Nazis, but German history provides a wealth of images and concepts for racists to exploit. Secondly, German-language Internet racism is global, and not limited to the German, Austrian and Swiss Internets. Just as American organisations are estimated to produce and send 85 per cent of all outlawed neo-Nazi propaganda, German-language Internet racism largely originates from North America.[6] Western Europe (predominantly the UK and Belgium) accounts for much of the rest of the foreign-generated German Internet racism.

The latest figures show that 16.4 per cent of the German population of 82 million has Internet access, and 47.3 per cent of households now own a computer.[7] Germany is now one of the most common addresses in the world-wide-web, having breached 5 million domain names. By early 2001, the suffix '.de' had become second only to '.com', and thus the most widely used country-specific

---

3. *Ibid*, p. 12. The other country was Sweden.
4. *Anti-Semitism Worldwide 1999/2000*, Stephen Roth Institute: http://www.tau.ac.il/anti-semitism/asw-2000/germany.htm. Former Internet monitor *Hatewatch* located nine German-language sites conforming to their category of 'hate-site', based on the presence of 'advocacy of violence against or unreasonable hostility toward a person or group based on race, religion, ethnicity, gender, sexual orientation or disability'.
5. *Annual Report of the Federal Office for the Protection of the Constitution 2000* (Cologne), p. 19. Available in German and English at http://www.verfassungsschutz.de/.
6. *Combating Right-wing Violence and Hate Crimes in Germany,* German Embassy Background Paper, Washington DC, 2000. Available at http://www.germany-info.org/f_index.html.
7. Statistics from the Federal Statistic Office, Germany available at http://www.statistik-bund.de.

domain in the world.[8] The German-language Internet can be broadly defined to include German-language material from Austrian and Swiss servers, and material from non-German speaking countries designed for a German-speaking audience. This paper will in the definition and analysis of German-language Internet racism therefore distinguish between sites emerging from Germany, where the publication of racist or antisemitic material, including Holocaust denial, is illegal, (referred to here as 'domestic material') and those originating from countries where legislation is less restrictive (termed 'foreign material').[9]

German 'Cultural Anxiety'

According to some commentators, Germany is experiencing a 'neo-Nazi crisis'.[10] Racist violence appears to have increased since reunification, and in particular its occurrence in rural eastern locations is of great concern. The total number of violent acts committed against non-Germans increased by almost 40 per cent in 2000: between January and November, a total of 13,753 acts of right-wing, xenophobic and antisemitic violence were registered, half of which took place in Eastern Germany (which is home to only 21 per cent of the population).[11] The Campaign Against Racism and Fascism (CARF) contends that Germany's racist culture is strongest in the Eastern border towns.[12] Meanwhile, Germans report the appearance of stickers bearing provocative anti-immigration slogans in small towns much further West.[13] Vandalism of Jewish cemeteries and attacks on both synagogues and asylum seekers resi-

8. DENIC Press Releases, 13th February 2001, and 5th November 2001 available at http://www.denic.de. DENIC also reported on 19th February 2002 that '.de' domains are almost exclusively registered to German users.

9. Unless otherwise indicated, all websites were located during the period September 2000—March 2001 and verified during February 2002.

10. *The Daily Telegraph*, Saturday 2nd December 2000. Austria and Switzerland have also recently had their own related crises due to a growth in the political strength of the far right. In Austria, electoral successes of the Freedom Party were strongest in the provinces bordering Slovenia. Switzerland voted in November 2000 to restrict numbers of immigrants to 18 per cent of its population.

11. *Die Woche*, 9th February 2001.

12. *Refugees from Globalism*, CARF 57, August/September 2000. Available at http://carf.demon.co.uk/feat30.html.

13. I am grateful to Beate Nettman-Roy, in Witten, near Dortmund, for this information.

dences continue in both Eastern and Western Germany, predominantly carried out by male youths of as young as 15 years old[14] In March 2001, the District Court in Mannheim convicted two musicians in the skinhead-band '*Bosheit*' of inciting crowds to violence against Jews.

This continued racist violence has prompted the government to introduce a wide range of counter measures. In 1994, new laws aimed at curtailing the growth in right-wing extremism and anti-foreigner violence were brought into force. This legislation broadened the definition of incitement of violence and racial hatred to include defamatory statements regarding whole groups and minorities and increased the penalties for crimes involving personal injury. It also improved police capacity for monitoring and investigating extremist activities. The Federal Office for the Protection of the Constitution currently monitors 120 extremist right-wing organisations in Germany and the three far-right political parties: the *Deutsche Volksunion*, the *Republikaner* and the *Nationaldemokratische Partei Deutschlands* (NPD). The Federal Constitutional Court is currently reviewing evidence of the NPD's affinity with Nazism to establish its unconstitutionality, following the party's implication in racist and antisemitic violence. An additional DM65 million towards its youth violence prevention program together with a rehabilitation program for known extremists who wish to leave the neo-Nazi movement was announced in February 2001. The government has also begun to tackle Internet racism as a source of xenophobic sentiment in Germany, notably via the Internet itself.[15]

Germany is a country that is uniquely placed, situated as it is on the former battle-line of the Cold War, to experience the growing pains of globalisation. Although officially 'not a country of immigration', the mass movement of people from East to West has twice been the major cause of defining moments in modern German history, namely the Potsdam agreement, and later both the building and tearing down of the Berlin Wall. Net immigration to the former *Bundesrepublik* was more than 18 million between 1945 and 1989 (compared to 16 million in the US).[16] In 1999 alone, 673,900 foreigners migrated to

14. As was the case in Mannheim in February 2001, when a group of three young men aged 15-17 attacked a Jewish cemetery.

15. The Federal Office for the Protection of the Constitution launched its web campaign against rightwing extremism in January 2001, urging Germans to show 'civil courage': http://www.verfassungsschutz.de/.

16. W.D. Chapin, *Germany for the Germans? The Political Effects of International Migration*, (Westport, 1997), xii.

Germany.[17] The Jewish community has been among those keen to leave the former Soviet Union, which has led to a tripling of Germany's Jewish population in the last ten years from 30,000 to 90,000.[18] This trend is unlikely to abate, as it is estimated that Germany will have to take in 140,000 immigrants annually for the next fifteen years to assure a steady labour supply.[19] Meanwhile the incentives for migrants from developing countries to pursue a higher standard of living in Western Europe are unlikely to go away. Although the Schengen agreement has created a 'Fortress Europe' keeping potential economic migrants at bay, Germany finds itself increasingly in need of skilled technical workers as its workforce diminishes through low birth rates and rising life-expectancy. Recognition of this prompted the introduction of US-style Green Card system in 2000. New laws on immigration aimed at reinforcing both the constitutional commitment to asylum for the persecuted, and ensuring that foreign non-EU professionals in scientific and technical fields can migrate to Germany are being hotly debated in the *Bundestag*. Immigration is widely expected to become an election issue when Germans go to the polls in September 2002.

The effects of globalisation and concepts of multiculturalism are thus very much in the public eye. In November 2000, Friedrich Merz, chair of the CDU political party, aroused controversy throughout Germany by introducing the concept of a German '*Leitkultur*' which new immigrants should adhere to. Still undefined in German, it has been taken to mean 'leading culture' or 'guiding culture', and has been widely challenged as being at the very least questionable and at most inherently xenophobic. Debate has focused on how to define German culture, and whether an attempt to define it is actually possible, with defendants claimed that the term describes the natural process by which immigrants adjust to a host culture.[20] More recently, the CDU/CSU candidate for Chancellor, Edmund Stoiber, has declared his strong dislike for the concept of Germany as a multicultural society.[21]

---

17. Statistics on cross-border migration from *The Debate on Immigration*, German Embassy, Background Paper, Washington DC, 2000. It should be noted that almost as many people (672,000) migrated *from* Germany.

18. ADL Anti-Semitism International press release, 31st July 2000. Available at http://www.adl.org.

19. *The Debate on Immigration*, German Embassy Background Paper, Washington DC, 2000. Available at http://www.germany-info.org/f_index.html.

20. *Ibid*.

21. Rightwing Bavarian joins race for Chancellor', *The Independent*, 12th January 2002.

Explaining Increases in Internet-based Racist Activity

The Internet is a window onto the world. Although admittedly not yet accessible to the majority of the world's population, and therefore not a truly global phenomenon, the Internet psychologically has the potential to make us feel that we are in a global village. This is a double-edged sword: while we gladly seek the exotic, we also are threatened by the intrusion of the unknown into the privacy of our own homes. In the following analysis, I will seek to show how the inherent nature of the medium itself may go some way to explaining the emergence and proliferation of anti-social attitudes and behaviour via the Internet.

When analysing the extent and nature of Internet material of any kind, the classification of websites is a crucial factor. There are obvious limitations to the assumptions we can make purely on the basis of quantitative data, especially the numbers of sites classified as far-right, fascist or extremist. In countries such as Germany, where incitement to racism is a crime, websites may fall short of these categories, but nonetheless be a critical part of building xenophobia. At the soft end of the spectrum we see sites that are devoted to military history, German history and patriotism as well as right-wing youth groups. These contain material that is unpleasant and are often linked to the more extreme sites, but cannot be defined as 'hate sites' in themselves.

It is easy to manipulate computer-based communication to achieve a misleading impression in terms of the size of a movement or quality of its activities. Small groups with large agendas will do their best to make their sites look professional and substantial when in fact they may be run out of the home study or even bedroom. Website creators are able to create a number of sites serving different purposes according to their different interests and identities. This is the case with Thomas Brookes, a well-known Holocaust denier, who is the publisher of the 'National Journal', a well-known revisionist site,[22] and also has a home page dedicated to honouring revisionist historians such as David Irving. Mr. Brookes expresses his more extreme views via the dynamic and updated 'National Journal', while reaching out to an uninitiated audience through the virtual and perpetual 'Hall of Heroes'.[23] With authorship easily

22. http://www.abbc.com/nj/. An English version is also available at http://www.abbc.com/nj/engl.htm. The National Journal is also sometimes available via http://www.globalfire.tv/nj.

23. http://www.aazz.com/tb/. Not available in February 2002.

made anonymous, seemingly diverse Internet sites with various international domains can be the amateur creation of one well-connected group or individual. In addition, the dynamic and unstable nature of the Internet means that a great number of websites are created and then abandoned, becoming quickly redundant and unseen.[24]

We are currently seeing an increase in everything on the Internet, and it is too early to predict whether this period of growth will last. In the context of the vast world-wide-web, racist material of either European or North American origin is still a minority aspect. There is a wealth of material produced by international and national bodies, as well as non-governmental organisations, aimed at educating and informing the public about human rights and the development of peaceful tolerant societies. By now, most established civil society organisations in the US and in Europe have a reasonably functioning website. These now share cyberspace with vast numbers of commercial sites which have sprung up as the Internet is promoted as a revolutionary tool for global business. But importantly, the business community has already noted a flattening out of the growth curve in e-commerce: dot.com businesses have notoriously failed on both sides of the Atlantic.[25] In addition, noting teenage boredom with the new medium in the UK during 2001, researchers at the Virtual Society claimed that the Internet is just another 'passing fad'.[26]

Internet technology appears to be spreading from West to East in a wave that reflects interest and activity. Behind the wave, people have recovered from the hype, but in front of the crest, the momentum is building. The price and availability of Internet connection is still high in Eastern Europe, particularly in the former Soviet Union. Given that there is still some way to go until individual homes are connected to the Internet, the peak of individual and associational Internet usage in Europe is still to come. There may come a point in the not-too-distant future, in which all active organisations, including those devoted to extremist activities, are on-line.

---

24. According to the Federal Office for the Protection of the Constitution 2000 Annual Report, homepages often deliberately change their storage locations in order to avoid being blocked, see p. 106.

25. According to the Guardian, 3rd March, 2001, dot.coms closed at a rate of more than one a day world-wide between December 2000 and February 2001.

26. See for example S. Wyatt, *They came, they surfed, they went back to the beach: why some people stop using the internet.* Virtual Society Report available at http://virtualsociety.sbs.ox.ac.uk.

Related to this point, as access to the Internet becomes easier and cheaper and people have the technology and know-how to create their own powerful websites from servers in their own homes, there is bound to be an increase in personal individual expression on the Internet. Racism monitors have noted that the most offensive forms of Internet racism are created by young individuals from their home computers.[27] The unregulated, anonymous nature of the Internet makes it an obvious choice for the expression of extreme views, especially the posting of controversial images. The Internet encourages not only personal expression, but perhaps also more uninhibited forms of communication as a reactive medium. The deceptive distance and paradoxical intimacy of virtual interaction has been recognised as a contributory factor in the high numbers of Internet libel cases since the mid-nineties.[28] More formal than a telephone conversation but less formal than a letter, email is a new mode of communication which has yet to develop codified or standardised rules and etiquette. Potential misunderstandings can arise from the absence of tone and other non-verbal indicators normally present in conversation. Sitting in front of a computer monitor, people are more likely via this medium to communicate rashly and hastily without considering the implications of their words or actions. The posting of provocative images and slogans can be interpreted as a virtual version of graffiti, and as with graffiti, it is hard to stop the perpetrators.

Many commentators have reflected on the ability to change one's identity on the Internet by virtue of the anonymity it allows. The opportunities for disadvantaged groups within society to use the Internet as a level playing field are clear.[29] While this is a positive development for many, it also offers the chance to take on an identity in the virtual world that is not appropriate in the real one, and express anger and even violence in a safe way. The emergence of sites aimed at teenagers explicitly providing virtual expressions of violence via email is a striking example of this.[30] Thus, despite its capacity to by-pass prejudice, the Internet is being exploited in a myriad of ways to promote it.

---

27. Confirmed by Neil Stevenson of the Race Equality Unit, Home Office.

28. L. Edwards and C. Waelde, *Law and the Internet: A Framework for Electronic Commerce*, (Oxford, 2000), 251.

29. As Gillian Youngs points out, the Internet 'hinders assumptions', in G. Youngs, *Virtual Voices: Real Lives* in W. Harcourt, *Women@internet* (London, 1999), 66.

30. For example, http://www.boesetaten.de.

The unique potential of the Internet for worldwide business and education has been well documented. Its diversity and flexibility offers some crucial advantages over other media. The Internet is a cheap and effective way of communicating to a very large audience. Unlike printed publication, a moderate investment in placing a site can be the only major cost involved. In theory, the chances of a casual surfer seeing your site is potentially higher than them glancing through a publication at the newsagent, although this is not always borne out in reality. Geography becomes insignificant. Even better, the Internet offers interactive elements so that communication can go both ways. It is not surprising that organisations with political agendas are interested in the new media capabilities: the ability to learn about your audience makes the Internet a potentially powerful community-building medium.

There are a number of advantages for extremists to use the unregulated Internet besides publishing illegal material, influencing opinion and recruiting new members. One example of how extremists are exploiting the technology is in their use of passwords on Internet sites for subscribers enabling them to gain access to more extreme material.[31] Given the difficulties of advertising such a service, access is presumably by word of mouth and not simply through the website. This is just one example of how racist sites are catering to an initiated and converted audience rather than reaching out to new recruits. Although not the focus of this paper, email has revolutionised communication methods and has played a role in most of the serious abuses of the new technology, for example the case in France of 500 antisemitic emails calling correspondents to 'put a 200-kilogram bomb' in the heart of the Jewish quarter in Paris.[32] Again, this illustrates how a minority of established extremists can exploit the Internet-based communication enjoyed by a vast majority of commercial and amateur users.

'Calling a Spade a Spade': Themes in Foreign German-language Material

The publication of racist and antisemitic material, including Holocaust denial, is banned in any media in Germany, Austria and Switzerland. In addition,

31. For example on Thule Net, http://www.thulenet.com.

32. *The Jewish Chronicle*, 15 December 2000.

the distribution and public use of Nazi memorabilia, including swastikas and other emblems from the Third Reich, have been illegal since 1945. As a result, German-language Holocaust denial and racial hatred is found (except in rare cases) on websites based abroad. This includes downloadable versions of *'Mein Kampf'* and the 'Protocols of the Elders of Zion' in German. A notable example is the North American site 'Thule Net' which promotes such material in a section entitled 'Content punishable by law: incitement and thought crimes'.[33] The creators of 'Thule Net' proudly announce that by placing material on a foreign server they can 'call a spade a spade' and elude German law. They are part of a growing number of European extremists switching to foreign, particularly US servers, to publish otherwise illegal material.

The neo-Nazi Gerhard Lauck is one such disseminator of illegal propaganda, through his organisation, NSDAPAO, explicitly created in 1972 for the purpose of providing the National Socialist underground in Germany with propaganda materials. Lauck was found guilty of inciting racial hatred by a German court in August 1996 and deported to the US in 1999 following a four-year sentence. From his base in Nebraska under the protection of the First Amendment, Lauck continues to spread Neo-Nazi propaganda over the Internet, including via German and English 'Internet radio'.[34] This 'radio' consists in fact of audio clips which can be downloaded and played using easily available and free software.

Foreign-based German-language extremism appears to emanate from a small number of prominent Holocaust deniers, whose sites are host to a wide array of extremist pages.[35] *'Wilhelm Tell'*, an extreme Swiss nationalist site, has been linked to the 'National Journal', run by Holocaust denier Thomas Brookes in Sussex, England.[36] Even the so-called 'Austrian' site, 'Ostara', a major source of German-language Holocaust denial, is based in California.[37] Holocaust denial is therefore a linking theme for all German-language racism originating outside Germany and Austria. German-language racism emerging from abroad deliberately targets both a German-speaking audience and the neo-Nazi movement as part of the project to re-establish far-right ideology

33. http://www.thulenet.com/strafbar/index.htm.
34. http://www.nazi-lauck-nsdapao.com.
35. I am grateful to Brian Hanrahan for research on Holocaust denial undertaken at the Centre for German-Jewish Studies in 1998-1999.
36. http://www.ety.com/tell.
37. http://www.ostara.org.

on a global scale. As Holocaust deniers have themselves admitted, attempts to rejuvenate National Socialism as a credible political movement have to begin with a revision of German history denying that the Holocaust took place.[38]

Of the White supremacist organisations aiming at an international audience, 'Stormfront' and 'Front14' are two of the largest which incorporate German-language material. Whereas Stormfront's German pages consist of a few text-heavy antisemitic documents, Front14 has previously focused more on acting as a host to international neo-Nazi groups. During 2001, it featured at least eight German-based users out of 104 members worldwide.[39] Notably two of these German sites made use of the Internet regulation in Germany stating that they are not automatically responsible for the content of websites that they are linked to.[40] A disclaimer distancing the content of all links through webrings or listed on links pages is enough to satisfy German law.

Wild conspiracy theories abound on the Internet, and racist material offers some of the most bizarre examples. On 'Thule Net', The Protocols of the Elders of Zion are linked with everything from immigration, through BSE and genetically modified foods to cannibalism. Under latest news on *'Wilhelm Tell'*, the UN is accused of planning the 'final solution for the White race' by encouraging the immigration of "159 million additional Africans and Asians to Western Europe by the year 2025". 'Scriptorium' is an on-line bookstore in English and German dedicated to presenting 'the other side of the coin' under the theme of 'German persecution since WW2', meaning the persecution of the German people.[41] This literature actually draws on the prevalence of conspiracy culture to suggest that the German government is brainwashing its citizens: 'What the German government calls democracy we call dictatorship of the mind... What they call multiculturalism, we call the genocide of European ethnicity'.[42] An even clearer example of this is found on Thomas Brookes' 'Hall of Heroes' site:

> If anyone doubts that the Orwellian world is now upon us and tightening its grip, we refer to one of Germany's renowned news pagers (*sic*), 'Welt am Sonntag' (Oct.

---

38. *Annual Report of the Federal Office for the Protection of the Constitution 2000*, p. 95.
39. http://www.front14.org/users.htm. Front14 is periodically unavailable due to hackers attacking the site.
40. Ruling of the Hamburg District Court, 12th May 1998.
41. http://www.iolaos.com/scriptorium.
42. http://www.thulenet.com.

25, 1998, p. 38), describing the situation in democratic Germany as follows: 'The thought-police of the correct political opinion', is spreading in Germany.[43]

Racist sites (or 'racialist sites' as they choose to call themselves), are now using benign advertising strategies to attract attention. 'Ostara' uses a pop-up 'quizlet' on the Holocaust asking one multiple-choice question: 'How many died at Auschwitz? Test the extent to which you have been brainwashed'. The results are shown as a bar chart, but no factual answer is given. Interactive strategies such as this have clearly been adopted from developments in e-commerce. Furthermore, extensive details on how to circumvent legislation, surf anonymously, reach blocked servers and even publicise extremist websites can also be found on 'Ostara' and other such sites.[44]

A landmark ruling by the Federal Court of Justice on 12th December 2000 has, however, made it possible at least in theory to prosecute authors of racist and antisemitic material despite location on foreign servers.[45] This ruling came from the case of Australian Fredrick Toben, who was prosecuted for statements made in an open letter to a German judge and for publishing Holocaust denial material on the 'Adelaide Institute' website on an Australian server.[46] German law can now be applied to material of international origin distributed via the Internet. Those who place material that incites racial hatred or promotes neo-Nazi Holocaust denial on Internet servers in foreign countries, which are accessible to Internet users in Germany, can be found guilty of disturbing the peace in Germany, even if the peace has not actually been disturbed.[47] Lawyers however remain divided over whether such assertions of racism or Holocaust denial anywhere in the world can come under German law when its only expression in Germany is via the Internet.

Reasonably safe from the recent revision of German law unless they venture to repeat Toben's mistake of blatantly drawing attention to his material on

43. http://www.aazz.com/tb/e/intro-e.htm.

44. Instructions on how to reach a blocked server are provided by Gerhard Lauck at http://www.nazi-lauck-nsdapao.com.

45. *Berliner Zeitung*, 13th December 2000.

46. http://www.adelaideinstitute.org/. The website is still up and running: 'In the meantime we have noted the original four million Auschwitz death figure has been reduced by Jean Claude Pressac to a maximum of 800,000. This in itself is good news because it means that around 3.2 million people never died at Auschwitz—a cause for celebration' (quote taken from the site on 18th March 2001).

47. This applies only in the case where the author places her or his own statements inciting racial hatred on the Internet, and does not apply to Internet Service Providers.

German soil, international propagandists continue with efforts to oppose and mobilise the public against Internet regulation. Many US sites display a Blue Ribbon as part of a campaign run by the Electronic Frontier Foundation in the US, dedicated to freedom of speech on all electronic media. This anti-censorship organisation is ostensibly devoted to fighting government restrictions on the use of computer technology, but through its prevalence on hate-sites risks being associated with less neutral aims.

'Unease Will Lead to Unrest'—Themes in Domestic Material

Indigenous German sites are for obvious reasons cautious about the level of extremism they present. It is hard to find explicit racism: instead, we find a more subtle cynicism and sarcasm.[48] References to religion and race are made in an ironic and suspicious tone, while the term multiculturalism, known as *'Multikulti'* in German slang, comes under explicit attack.[49] Immigration is posited as a threat to German identity and culture. The threat of violent response, however, is only thinly veiled. In the German site *'Die Kommenden'*,[50] we find a surprisingly honest admission in an opening homepage with a man in a balaclava: *'Aus Angst wird Wut, dann Widerstand—der Freiheit gilt's für dieses Land!'*—'From unease will come anger and then resistance—freedom is at stake for our country!'. This old-fashioned grammatical construction is a pertinent example of the revival of traditional and even ancient prejudices in the new media.

Among the predominant themes found in domestic material is a claim that an authoritarian Federal government is persecuting rightwing opinion and abusing human rights, notably the right to free speech. Related to this is

48. The EUMC has found that "racist discourse in 2000 is increasingly becoming implicit rather than explicit". See *Diversity and Equality for Europe, Annual Report 2000* (European Monitoring Centre on Racism and Xenophobia, Vienna, 2000), 13.
49. German radio station *'Radio MultiKulti'* offers Turkish language programs.
50. http://www.die-kommenden.net. Roughly translated the name of this site is 'the coming ones', acting as a statement of intention. The author has been unable to establish where this site is registered. It has been classified as domestic in origin due to the German nationality of the site's creators.

an anti-establishment critique bordering on conspiracy theory, and an oppositional stance towards the EU, NATO and other international bodies. Above all, indigenous material focuses on globalisation, with anti-Americanism as a prominent ideological theme.[51] The *'Die Kommenden'* site features photos of 'members' at rallies, protesting against multiculturalism, the EU and NATO but also calling for tolerance and freedom of speech. One of these photos is of demonstrators wielding a yellow flag with the word 'Nazi' encircled by the Star of David. We are told that police confiscated this immediately—yet it remains untouched on the website.

Neo-Nazis are known to have been among the quickest to adopt the Internet as a means of covert communication.[52] In 1999, the German authorities identified at least 16 'National Information Telephones' (NIT) which were being used to relay details of events and other information.[53] This system had established itself on the Internet as a well-designed and neat website calling itself 'News, Information, Theory' (similarly NIT) offering news items on far-right concerns, such as court cases involving racist crimes and the fate of the NPD.[54] The site even enabled viewers with basic audio equipment to hear these telephone announcements. However, by early 2002 this website was no longer in operation under the name NIT, reflecting the fluctuating success of such efforts.

German right-wing media have also been quick to go online and sometimes push the boundaries of what is legal. An important example is *'Nation und Europa'*, a subscription journal regarded as the leading publication dealing with right-wing extremist theory and strategy.[55] The November/December 2000 edition featured articles on *'Leitkultur'* and 'The Germans, A Dying Race'. According to the contributors, other countries have realised that the free movement of people is not desirable and that Germany is holding onto 'the madness of multicultural society'. Through its Internet presence, *'Nation und Europa'* is able to reach a much larger audience.[56] Also capitalising on the com-

---

51. *Annual Report of the Federal Office for the Protection of the Constitution 2000*, p. 41.

52. M. Whine, *Cyberspace, a new medium for Communication, Command and Control by Extremists*, (Studies in Conflict and Terrorism, RAND), p. 2. Available at http://www.ict.org.il/articledet.cfm?articleid=76.

53. *The State of Right-wing extremism in Germany*, Federal Office for the Protection of the Constitution, Cologne 2000. Available at http://www.verfassungsschutz.de/.

54. http://www.nit.de/. Not available in February 2002.

55. *Annual Report of the Federal Office for the Protection of the Constitution 2000*, p. 104.

56. http://www.nationeuropa.de.

mercial potential of the Internet, *'Rock Nord'* is just one of the many European music distributors that cater for the skinhead and racist punk scene under categories such as *'Rechtsrock'* (rightwing rock) and *'Patriotik-Rock'* (patriotic rock).[57] Skinhead music has been identified by the German government as a 'gateway' to rightwing extremism by establishing and consolidating groups of young men, with concerts acting as important meeting places.[58] Skinhead music is also known to be a major source of income for extremist organisations. Indeed, the EUMC reported recently that the right-wing music scene has become increasingly central to the activities of right-wing extremist groups.[59]

There is a prevalence of history sites and web-rings on the German web. A major example is the 'Geschichtsring Deutschland' web-ring run by Yahoo. Affirming national history is one of the principal elements of nationalism and there are a number of military history sites in these web-rings which have an ambiguous ideology, for example the now defunct website 'Drittes Reich' (Third Reich).[60] The Third Reich website disappeared from the Internet in 2001, presumably due to its offensive title. An individual homepage, ostensibly created by a young person interested in that period of history, it featured a disclaimer on the homepage distancing itself from National Socialism, and stating that the depiction of symbols is purely for purposes of authenticity and not propaganda. Here the question is whether a site devoted to the Nazi regime is, by default, promoting its values—the creator leaves it up to the viewer to decide.

There are some interesting linkages between sites on the right-wing spectrum: for example a site dedicated to Rudolf Hess links to the Imperial War Museum, while '*Nation und Europa*' links to the Federal Office for the Protection of the Constitution.[61] Lists of extreme far-right parties and personalities throughout Europe are not uncommon on these sites. More ominously, '*Die Kommenden*' provides the names of any youth club in Germany, Austria and Switzerland that might remotely be seen as left wing.[62] The ostensibly respect-

57. http://www.rocknord.de.
58. *Verfassungsschutz Gegen Rechtsextremismus*, Federal Office for the Protection of the Constitution, Cologne 2000. Available at http://www.verfassungsschutz.de/.
59. *Diversity and Equality for Europe: Annual Report 2000* (European Monitoring Centre on Racism and Xenophobia, Vienna, 2000), 12.
60. http://drittesreich.here.de—no longer available in February 2002.
61. http://rudolfhess.org and http;//www.nationeuropa.de
62. My thanks to Karin von Wartburg, MA Sussex for confirming that some of these youthclubs do not claim any exclusive political affiliation.

able on-line magazine '*Junge Freiheit*' for German rightwing youth is listed on several sites as either extremist or as anti-immigrationist, reciprocally offering links to '*Nation und Europa*.' A recent article warned that Europe will have to prepare itself for a new wave of immigrants. However, it has also featured a sophisticated and intelligent interview with the leader of the Jewish community in Bremen, Elvira Noa, on reported increases in youth violence.[63] Unlike foreign-based sites, the actual authorship and editorialship of German sites is more likely to be kept anonymous, and in contrast to the foreign-based sites, there is rarely an invitation to contact the site via email. Often technically more professional than foreign sites, given their aim for moderation, they avoid the alienating features found on more extremist web-sites. The openness of '*Junge Freiheit*', in showing full colour pictures of its production team, besides full contact details, for example, would suggest that it rests on the fringes of far-right opinion, no doubt unwittingly providing an entryway to illegal material.

The considered analysis of German-language racist sites reveals a small number of closely-related subjects recurring in domestic and foreign material. Both types of material are aimed at a European audience concerned about questions of national identity and culture in a time of imminent EU expansion and liberalisation of the global economy bringing change to economic production and labour migration patterns. Strikingly similar language is found on the '*Die_Kommenden*' and '*Thule Net*' sites, but the language is stronger on the latter. German-based sites are in many instances operating as gateways to foreign sites both literally through links pages but also psychologically by introducing Internet audiences to a blending of conspiracy theory, immigration scare-mongering and a patriotic rendition of German history.

The fairground mirror

Racism is an unwanted but persistent phenomenon in 21st century society, and we should not be surprised to see its expression via this new and dynamic media. However, it can be argued that the distinction between the real and the virtual should not be blurred. The Internet is like a mirror that 'tends to reflect society, not shape it',[64] in many ways a reflection of the world we live in, but its reflective

63. http://www.jungefreiheit.de/.

64. The net is not to blame for the Soho nail bomber, we are', *The Guardian*, 6th June 2000.

capacity is imperfect: we have a fairground mirror effect. It is therefore important not to gauge the extent of racist sentiment in Germany from a perceived prevalence of Internet sites. It is easy to assume from Internet-based statistics and research that the united German public is becoming increasingly intolerant. When taken together with Germany's recent history, they can misleadingly lend weight to the idea that the German people are inherently racist and antisemitic, and should be used with caution. Indeed, such interpretations risk feeding into the xenophobia found in Germany's neighbours, including Britain.

For every headline announcing a growth in xenophobic sentiment, there is a strong counter-response from the German people: 30,000 people demonstrated against the NPD in Berlin on 9th November 2000. At the same time as we are witnessing the development of racism, we are also seeing a huge increase in the numbers of people involved in progressive social activism, on- and off-line. The continued, if sometimes unhealthy, interest in the Nazi period and the Holocaust demonstrates the importance of the subject to society today. Beyond a remembrance of World War II, this interest seems to be connected to understanding the persistent occurrence of hatred and intolerance within all societies.

The emergence of some 800 German-based racist sites since the 1990's demonstrates a reaction to the process of globalisation and related multiculturalism of society. The '*Angst*' caused by dramatic change in former East and West Germany is finding expression on the Internet and on the street. We are faced with the possibility of an unholy alliance of minority extremists who seek to re-establish the political credibility of far-right ideology in Europe and elsewhere by denying the Holocaust, and a disenchanted public ready to protest over the rapid change that characterises the globalised world. Unease is the where extremism begins and this is where counter-efforts should be focused. However, while the unease of those in positions of prestige and influence is clearly an integral part of the creation of racism, we must not minimalise the far more crippling 'permanent angst' experienced by new residents in European communities as they face xenophobic violence on a daily basis.[65] It is both notable and encouraging that community websites for these global villagers are a part of the recent surge in German Internet usage.[66]

---

65. Quote from the spokesperson for the Islamic student community in Greifswald, East Germany, in an article by Christopher Seils, 'Zonen der Angst', *Die Woche*, 9 February 2001.

66. See for example http://www.islam.de/ and http://www.multikulti.de/.

The European Race Directive: A Bridge so Far?

Fernne Brennan*

On the 29th June 2000, the European Council of Ministers adopted Council Directive 2000/43/EC (Race Directive)[1] implementing the principle of equal treatment between persons irrespective of racial or ethnic origin.[2] The purpose of this directive is to lay down a common framework, for combating racial or ethnic discrimination in the Member States of the European Union.[3] The object of this common framework is to enable Member States to deliver an anti-race discrimination regime by putting into effect the principle of 'equal treatment'[4] in their domestic laws, regulations and administrative provisions.[5] Individuals[6] who consider themselves wronged may rely on national provi-

---

* *Lecturer in law, University of Essex*

1. Directives are binding on Member States to whom they are addressed, Article 254(3) EC.
2. Official Journal L 180, 19/07/2000 p. 0022-0026.
3. Council Directive 2000/43/EC, Article 1.
4. *Ibid.*
5. *Ibid.* Article 14.
6. The directive does not cover difference of treatment of third country nationals where their legal status has not been resolved at the level of national law. See Article 3(2) of Council Directive 2000/43/EC.

Raphael Walden (ed.), Racism and Human Rights, *143-164.*

sions brought in to give effect to the Race Directive. In this way, the European Community's promise[7] to provide measures to combat racism in the EU can start to take shape.

The use of a directive as an instrument to provide minimum protection for victims of racial discrimination is useful. The adoption of such a tool takes account of the divergent legal and cultural systems of different member states when pursuing the principle of equal treatment. By its nature a directive imposes obligations only on member states,[8] to achieve the end whilst leaving them choice as to form and method.[9] This choice of form and method enables account to be taken of the social and political differences provided member states review and/or create instruments that will enable them to ensure compliance with a directive.[10] Member states have until 19 July 2003 to complete the processes necessary to ensure that the directive will be complied with.[11]

The scope of the Race Directive covers employment, vocational training, working conditions, membership of workers or professional organisations, social protection, healthcare, social advantages, education and access to and supply of goods and services available to the public, including public housing.[12] The directive requires that member states remove racial and ethnic barriers in these areas in order to achieve the objectives of the EC Treaty such as a high level of employment, social protection, a better quality of life, and economic and social cohesion and inclusion.

The question for this paper is whether such a general legal instrument could be deployed as a model of 'good' practice for the development of appropriate worldwide mechanisms aimed at the eradication of racism and

7. Article 13 Treaty of Amsterdam amending the EC Treaty.

8. See Article 249(2) EC Treaty and Case 148/78. *Publico Ministero* v. *Tullio Ratti* [1979] ECR 1629.

9. Article 249(2) EC Treaty.

10. Once they are implemented, individuals can rely on the rights that they confer as against those who flout those rights. Individuals may rely on an unimplemented directive under the doctrines of 'direct effect', Case 41/74 *Van Duyn* v *Home Office* [1974] ECR 1337, [1975] 1 CMLR 1, and 'indirect effect' Case 14/83 *Von Colson and Kaman* v *Land Nordrhein-Westfalen* [1984] ECR 1891, [1986] 2 CMLR 430. They may also bring an action in damages against a Member State that fails to implement a directive Cases C-6/90 and C-9/90 *Francovich and Bonifaci* v *Italy* [1991] ECR I-5357, [1993] 2 CMLR 66.

11. Article 16 Council Directive 2000/43/EC.

12. *Ibid.* Article 3(1)(a)-(h).

racial discrimination. Are the common framework model, and the principle that it has been designed to fulfil, namely the equal treatment principle as a desired goal in the eradication of racism and racial discrimination, useful in this regard? In order to answer that question this paper intends to look at the viability of the directive by applying its operation to some of the 'racial' problems that continue to trouble the relatively divergent member states of the EU. The result of this practical application may provide some insight into the viability of 21st century common framework instruments, like the Race Directive, for providing a bridge across some of the problems associated with racism and racial discrimination. This paper will attempt to examine the potential operation of the directive in the context of a number of areas—racism, racial discrimination and mechanisms of support.

The Eradication of Racism

European Community institutions such as the European Monitoring Centre[13] state that racism is a multifaceted phenomenon.[14] According to the Commission for Racial Equality (CRE) in Britain, 'racism is the belief that some 'races' are superior to others—based on the false idea that different physical characteristics (such as skin colour) or ethnic background makes some people better than others.'[15] It takes many forms and may be expressed in a number of ways across the various member states, but 'racism and xenophobia is universal. No country in the Union is immune'.[16] European Community-wide studies carried out by scholars such as Ford[17] show that hatred of 'foreigners' has led to murderous killings of members of the Turkish, Roma and Iranian communities in Germany,[18] assassinations, and the physi-

---

13. Set up in accordance with Council Regulation No 1035/97 of June 2 1997 to monitor and report on racism and xenophobia in the Member States of the European Community.

14. European Monitoring Centre, *Looking Reality in the Face. Annual Report 1998* (Vienna, EUMC, 1998) p. 4.

15. See CRE , *What is Discrimination?'*, www.cre.uk/legaladv/rra_discrim.html

16. *Ibid*, p. 3.

17. G. Ford, *Report drawn up on behalf of the Committee of Inquiry into Racism and Xenophobia* (Luxembourg, Office of Official Publication of EC 1991).

18. *Ibid*, Ford, p. 57.

cal and mental handicapping of North Africans and Romanians in France.[19] Similarities can be drawn in Britain.[20] At the other end, there is general intimidation and harassment of 'foreigners' and suggestion by some Eurobarometer opinion polls that approximately 40% of people are racist.[21] That is not to say that racism is generally tolerated in member states. Numerous campaigns from governmental and non-governmental entities show that many ordinary people believe that racism is unacceptable and would not subscribe to it. Nevertheless, the existence of an unacceptable level of tolerance of racism and the failure of member states to adequately deal with it has prompted the European Community to legislate on a community wide level for its eradication.

The Race Directive attempts to deal with racism by making harassment a ground for legal action. Article 2(3)[22] states that

> Harassment shall, be deemed to be discrimination ...when any unwanted conduct related to racial or ethnic origin takes place with the purpose or effect of violating the dignity of a person and of creating an intimidating, hostile, degrading, humiliating or offensive environment.

It may be argued that this provision serves a dual function. One is the legislative function whilst the other relates to an educative function. In relation to the legislative function, this provision seeks to put in place a concept of racial or ethnic harassment as a legal concept. The implementation of laws, rules and sanctions regarding the concept of harassment must be, 'effective, proportionate and dissuasive'.[23] What this provision purports to do is to articulate the experience of victims of racial or ethnic harassment as one that must be addressed by the legal and administrative systems of member states. For the European Community, this is a relatively revolutionary move. There is the recognition that victims of racial or ethnic discrimination are often also victims of racial or ethnic harassment, and, to effectively deal with racial or ethnic discrimination, one must recognise the often hidden, debilitating effects of racial or ethnic harassment. Sniggering, name-calling, and racially motivated physical assaults are just as likely to lead to social exclusion as racially discrimina-

---

19. *Ibid*, Ford, p. 61-64.
20. See EUMC *op. cit.* p. 21.
21. *Ibid*, p. 22.
22. EC Directive 2000/43/EC.
23. Article 15 Council Directive 2000/43/EC.

tory job recruitment. In the English case of *Jones v Tower Boots*[24] for instance, the applicant was seriously harassed at work. Incidents included burning his arm with a hot screwdriver, throwing metal bolts at his head and racial verbal abuse. It may well be the case that in countries such as Germany and France, where racially motivated harassment is not properly recognised, a general legal requirement to link racial harassment to the right to be treated equally at work and in other sectors might bear fruit.[25]

The duty imposed on member states to produce the legal and administrative mechanisms to articulate racial or ethnic harassment as a legal concept also serves an educative function, raising awareness of the damage that can be caused by racial or ethnic harassment and imposing on human conduct certain limits. The more people know that the law prohibits certain kinds of behaviour, it is assumed, the less likely they are to infringe the law by behaving in ways that contravene such principles. Whether or not that is true, it is presumed that the law has a role in guiding human conduct and in this respect, the law is to guide conduct away from racial and ethnic harassment.

Legal prohibition of harassment as a right with the concomitant obligations may well serve as a useful universal principle; however, the provision for harassment falls far short of the type of prohibition against racism one would have expected the EC to provide. Given the wealth of material on the persistence of racially motivated violent and intimidating conduct in the various member states,[26] how far will a provision for legal harassment as unlawful racial or ethnic discrimination go to deter potential aggressors? Further, the provision does not require that racially motivated assaults should be subject to the national criminal law.[27] The limited recognition of racism in the guise of harassment is insufficient since it only has the potential to deal with low-level forms of racially motivated unwanted conduct e.g. verbal abuse, racist jokes

---

24. [1997] IRLR 168, CA.

25. For other examples see Council of Europe, *Second Report on Denmark*, Adopted 16 June 2000, COE Portal, Intranet and Council of Europe, *Second Report on Austria,* Adopted 16 June 2000, COE Portal, Intranet. Both countries have been criticised for the scope of their criminal provisions concerning racially motivated crimes.

26. See Report of the European Parliament, *On Countering Racism and Xenophobia in the European Union—Committee on Citizens' Freedoms and Rights, Justice and Home Affairs. Combating Racism and Xenophobia in the European Union,* A5-0049/2000, p. 6. B.

27. Subjecting racist conduct to criminal law raises a number of issues. There is a proposal for a Council Framework decision on combating racism and xenophobia (COM(2001) 664-C5-0689/2001—2001/0207(CNS)).

low level assaults etc. This is a major limitation. In Germany, for instance, much of the Turkish population bears the brunt of racial harassment, violence and discrimination and is relatively defenceless.[28] There has been a rise in racially motivated attacks against them and others such as asylum seekers, Jews, Africans and Vietnamese.[29] According to Horrocks and Kolinksy,[30] German unification brought with it dire consequences for those seen as the *Auslanderproblem,* i.e., problems caused by the presence of foreigners,[31] more racist and xenophobic assaults and murders. Whilst banning some neo-Nazi groups and passing harsher sentences on right-wing extremist offenders calmed the situation many Germans still see the solution as one of exclusion. Turkish people (as well as other minority communities) are negatively portrayed in German culture, in anti-Turkish computer games and in everyday discourse and behaviour of ordinary young Germans.[32] No doubt, some of this is fuelled by racist ideology that portrays Turkish people as homogeneous, monochrome, culturally backward and an underclass brainwashed by Islamic fundamentalism.[33] This is far from the truth. In France people from the Maghreb (western parts of North Africa consisting of Algeria, Morocco and Tunisia) and the Asian communities experience similar problems with racism that goes beyond racial harassment. There is evidence to suggest that some of this antagonism is fuelled by the myth that the African Muslim will not be able to 'integrate'.[34] Integration in this context means that they will not assimilate to 'French norms'.[35] It could be argued that member states should have had positive obligations to ensure that their criminal justice systems adequately deal with racially motivated attacks.[36] This might include identifying certain

28. Ford, *op. cit.* p. 57.

29. D. Horrocks and E. Kolinsky, eds, *Turkish Culture in German Society Today* (Oxford, Berghahn Books, 1996), p. 104.

30. D. Horrocks, *op. cit.*

31. D. Horrocks, *op. cit.* p. 104.

32. *Ibid.* p. xii.

33. *Ibid.* p. xx.

34. C. Wihtol de Wenden, "North African Immigration and the French Political Imaginary", in M. Silverman (ed), *Race, Discourse and Power in France* (Aldershot, Avebury, 1991), pp. 98-109.

35. *Ibid.*

36. There are arguments that the identification of crimes on the basis of 'race' or 'ethnicity' is likely to raise more problems than it is likely to solve. See F. Brennan, 'Racially Motivated Crime: the Response of the Criminal Justice System' (1999) Crim L. R, 17-28.

types of conduct as race/hate crimes across all the member states and requiring that criminal sanctions (as well as the right to civil action) be imposed. The legal recognition of harassment as prohibited conduct could usefully feed into a universal mechanism but it is not enough. A universal instrument needs to take proper legal account of the range of racially motivated conduct and commensurate criminal penalty.[37]

Another limitation that occurs with the harassment provision is its reliance on the concept of racial or ethnic discrimination, rather than standing alone as a separate provision. According to Article 2(3) *Harassment shall be deemed to be discrimination within the meaning of paragraph 1.*[38] Essentially this means that racial or ethnic harassment will be recognised as covered by the directive only where it is connected with racial or ethnic discrimination, rather than where it is a manifestation of racism per se since paragraph 1 requires that the directive '*...is to lay down a framework for combating discrimination on the grounds of racial or ethnic origin...*'[39] The concept of discrimination requires that the perpetrator's conduct is either motivated by unlawful discrimination (direct discrimination) or that the perpetrator's conduct is 'reckless' and that it is this thoughtlessness that leads to discrimination (indirect discrimination). If neither of these states of mind exists on the part of the perpetrator then, arguably, harassment cannot be proved even though the person has suffered from harassing conduct. The harassment provision also raises questions about the standard of proof that is required to show that harassment type conduct is racially or ethnically motivated. Without common guidance as to standard, the requisite evidence is likely to vary and dilute the effectiveness of this provision. As a universal principle attention has to be paid to such matters.

Nevertheless, the requirement on the part of member states to implement provisions that focus on discriminatory racial or ethnic harassment is likely to go some way toward resolving the problem of racially motivated conduct. Low-level type racially motivated harassment will no longer be tolerable or tolerated. In a number of member states notably France and Germany racism is seen as a taboo subject and there is a failure to connect racial or ethnic har-

---

37. Now see the Proposal for a *Council Framework Decision on Combating Racism and Xenophobia*, COM (2000) 664 final, Brussels, 28.11.2001, the purpose of which is to ensure that racism and xenophobia are punishable in all Member States and to improve judicial cooperation.

38. Council Directive 2000/43/EC.

39. *Ibid.* Art 1.

assment with anything other than that promulgated by the Far Right. This leads to the assumption that arguments about the lack of integration of Muslims in France or for the preservation of German culture for ethnic Germans are separate, legitimate pursuits that have nothing to do with racial harassment. A number of Germans associate racism with Nazism and fascism. Accordingly, there is a tendency not to associate certain types of conduct targeted against Turkish peoples, asylum seekers etc as racist, but rather to see it is an inevitable consequence of 'uncontrolled' immigration. Harassment at least focuses the minds of member states' towards the manifestation of racism and, perhaps more importantly, what can be done to counter it.

In France there is a long tradition of cultural cohesion premised on the principles of '*jus sanguinis*' (mixing) and '*jus soli*' (entitlement to citizenship).[40] The concept of integration is premised on the notion that people who originate from outside of France will assimilate.[41] If they do not they should repatriate. The French history of its relationship with the Maghreb is peppered with government policies aimed at turning on the tap of migration from the Maghreb when it suited its need for labour shortage and closing it with repatriation when the need for labour shortage declined.[42] The ideology surrounding the way such peoples were recruited was based on racist-oriented policy. Hargreaves argues that whilst the Vietnamese 'boat people' were received as victims of political intolerance with valuable entrepreneurial skills, Africans have been portrayed as economic, non-deserving asylum seekers and received with hostility.[43] The way in which political systems have helped to cultivate and maintain in place ideas and practices that make it easier for harassment to occur may be put under the legislative microscope by a universal prohibition against harassment. What the harassment provision does is to obligate member state to attention on those places where this process is likely to occur and force them to provide some means by which victims can bring action and seek compensation from the perpetrators.

40. A.C. Hargreaves, *Immigration, 'Race' and Ethnicity in Contemporary France* (London, Routledge, 1995).

41. *Ibid.* p. 2.

42. *Ibid.* p. 15-20.

43. *Ibid.* p. 21.

Racial or Ethnic Discrimination

The directive provides that, '*...there shall be no direct or indirect discrimination based on racial or ethnic origin.*'[44] Rather European citizens are to be treated equally according to the principle of 'equal treatment.' The prohibition of discrimination includes conduct and practices motivated by racial or ethnic preference (direct discrimination)[45] as well as the conduct that may hide or not set out to discriminate, but nevertheless end up doing so (indirect discrimination).[46] The only principle upon which job selection, housing allocation, service provision etc is to be allocated is the principle of equal treatment.

The principle of equal treatment is a familiar legal concept in the context of Community law aimed at the elimination of gender-based discrimination. Here the essence of equal treatment from the European Community perspective tends to be that of equality of opportunity: the right to be treated equally regardless of gender.[47] If equality of opportunity is what is envisaged by the principle of equal treatment contained in the Race Directive then it is likely to be based on this type of merit principle. Bercusson[48] argues that the familiar concept employed in European Community law—the merit principle—is based on a notion of formal equality that emphasises the need for everyone to be allowed to compete on an equal footing. Race and ethnicity are deemed by the directive to be irrelevant criteria.[49] The directive perceives EC citizens as people who have the right to pursue the objectives of the Community such as employment, a raised standard of living and social protection[50] without being subject to racial or ethnic discrimination which is seen as undermining such objectives.[51]

The principle of equal treatment irrespective of race or ethnicity can be seen as providing a mechanism for challenging employment policy and prac-

---

44. Article 2(1) Council Directive 2000/43/EC.
45. Article 2(2)(a) Council Directive 2000/43/EC.
46. Article 2(2)(b) Council Directive 2000/43/EC.
47. Case C-450/930 *Kalanke* v *Freie Hansestadt Bremen* [1995] ECR I-3051.
48. B. Bercusson, *European Labour Law* (Butterworths, London, 1996), p. 174-180.
49. Except insofar as they are relevant to 'genuine occupational qualifications' or to 'positive action programmes', see Articles 4 and 5 respectively of the Council Directive 2000/43/EC.
50. See para 9 of Council Directive 2000/43/EC.
51. See para 9 of Council Directive 2000/43/EC.

tice across a number of member states that tend to marginalise people to the least powerful, most exploited and least secure areas of the labour market. For instance, Palmer, Moon and Cox[52] write that in Britain many black and Asian people are disadvantaged in the labour market because of the way they were recruited to the British labour market. Africans and Afro-Caribbean's came as seamen and cheap forms of labour from the colonies and ex-colonies. In the post-war period, many were recruited into the less 'skilled' poorly paid jobs such as public transport and nursing to help with the reconstruction of Britain. It is still the case that despite the settlement of such people in Britain many occupy the lower rungs of the job market and are more likely to experience the ravages of unemployment. Recent information regarding the Bangladeshi and Pakistani communities in Oldham, north of England suggests that there is 40% unemployment, they are placed in the worst types of housing and have become a target for neo-nazi groups. Further, argues Jones,[53] despite the highest of qualifications, Afro-Caribbean men are more likely than whites to be in lower valued jobs.

Scholars writing in the context of France with the Maghreb and the Turkish community in Germany have reported similar experiences of racially discriminatory labour markets. Hargreaves[54] points out that in France there are, '... patterns of social differentiation marked by discriminating behaviour against people of foreign origin.'[55] Hargreaves argues that in France, as in Britain, the somatic differences (i.e. bodily) of people of third world origin frequently arouse exclusionary attitudes. Similarly, people from 'minority' communities in Germany tend to occupy the lower echelons of the employment market. Kolinsky[56] contends that in terms of social exclusion criteria such as low income, homelessness, unemployment and poverty, resident non-Germans suffered far worse than West or East Germans on all accounts. This is partly due to the recruitment policy in Germany, particularly towards the Turkish community, which has tended to treat Turkish people as a temporary and cheap source labour.

---

52. Palmer, Moon and Cox, *Discrimination at Work* (London, LAG, 1997), pp. 6-9.
53. T. Jones, *Britain's Ethnic Minorities: An analysis of the Labour Force Survey,* (London, Policy Studies Institute, 1996).
54. Hargreaves, *op. cit.*
55. Hargreaves, *op. cit.* p. 32.
56. E. Kolinsky, *op. cit.* p. 100.

One of the problems, then, that the prohibition of racial discrimination in labour has to effect is patterns of employment in the EU that maintain systems of cheap labour based on race or ethnicity. By implication, employers should also open up all employment markets to competition based on the merit principle alone. In that way, jobs would be filled only on the basis of competence.

The duty not to discriminate on the basis of race or ethnicity is arguably morally sound, but how is this to work in practice? Apparent problems are that merit criteria may not be the only criteria important to employers. In certain markets, particularly the less skilled ones, employers concerns may be with the *cost* of labour rather than *somatic* differences. Recruitment then may reflect economies of scale rather than intentional racial discrimination. Where an employer shows this then it can be argued that there is no racial or ethnic discrimination, despite what the recruitment market 'looks like'. Labour markets that tend to have sectors where cheap labour is primarily ethnic minority labour may be a reflection of the ability of employers to maximise capital by recruiting from the cheapest source. It is not necessarily the case that employers deliberately recruit and maintain systems of cheap and insecure employment on the basis of race, rather on the basis of cost. The principle of equal treatment cannot tap into this problem on its own. Additional measures need to be taken on board that will tackle such problems. The Directive does not appear to provide for the resolution of such difficulties. A universal provision would need to take this on board.

It could be argued that the language of 'cost' is a disguised and arbitrary means of maintaining and racialising markets. The sooner legal language is developed to deal with this the better. There is provision in the directive for indirect or disparate discrimination. Accordingly, '...*where an apparently neutral provision, criterion or practice would put persons of a racial or ethnic origin at a particular disadvantage compared with other persons...*'[57] such conduct is prohibited. This provision would seem to take care of the concern expressed by many scholars and organisations that third country nationals may be exploited by employment practices in the West. Employers may deploy criteria, which prohibit such peoples from taking up the more lucrative posts, forcing them to rely on cheaper, less secure alternatives. By imposing requirements such as language, knowledge of local customs and culture etc, which are neither 'essential' nor 'desirable' criteria for posts, such criteria tends to favour certain 'groups' and present obstacles to others.

57. Article 2(2)(b) Council Directive 2000/43/EC.

However, there is provision for employers to fall back on such exclusionary criteria if it can be shown that the, '... *provision, criterion or practice is objectively justified by a legitimate aim and the means of achieving that aim are appropriate and necessary.*'[58] Whilst there needs to be some balance between the needs of industry and that of labour this provision is likely to prove contentious. Anderman[59] has argued in the context of gender equality that such a provision whilst neutral on its face serves to diminish the protective thrust of the legislation since it maintains the institutionalised patterns of discrimination between men and women.[60] In the context of the institutionalised patterns of discrimination that have been identified in the EU towards peoples from the third world, it is unfortunate that the Community has sought to maintain in place the 'objective justification' criteria in Article 2 rather than a more stringent and balanced test. This is an area that, in terms of a universal principle, requires a measure that is more penetrating.

Whilst the directive fails to deal adequately with patterns of employment that are not necessarily based on direct of indirect racial or ethnic discrimination, but nevertheless tends to structure markets along those lines, the potential exits to challenge the more overt forms of racial and ethnic discrimination that clearly do exist in a number of member states. Employers will be under a duty to ensure that they do not discriminate in the way they recruit, and, where there is evidence of discrimination, claimants have the right to ask the courts to provide them with a remedy. Potentially, this is a powerful weapon in the hands of those who may experience the sharper end of racial and ethnic discriminatory employment practices.

The Meaning of Race/Ethnicity

The Race Directive is peppered with the words 'race' and 'ethnicity', indeed these words are part of its driving force yet there is no definition provided of what these terms mean. We are told that they do not refer to origins or separate races, '*The European Union rejects theories which attempt to determine the exis-*

58. Article 2(2)(b).

59. S. Anderman, 'Constitutional Law and Labour Law. Dimensions of Article 119: The Case of Justification for Indirect Discrimination', in J. Dine and B. Watt, *Discrimination Law. Concepts, Limitations and Justifications* (London, Longman, 1996).

60. *Ibid*, p. 109.

tence of separate human races. The use of the term "racial origin" in this Directive does not imply an acceptance of such theories.'[61] So what do these terms mean and how are they to be understood when interpreting the directive? Moreover, how are these terms to provide an all-embracing framework for dealing with racism and racial/ethnic discrimination?

The European Community is concerned to get away from biologically determined notions of racial origin. This is in part due to the influence of eugenics and theories of inferior races that have tended to serve the interests of Western Imperial powers. The notion that third world people are inferior to those in the West would not fit with the moral and human rights culture that has evolved in the West. However, there is another consideration. Given the 'historical mix' of various populations over the centuries it makes no sense to talk of or think in terms of 'race' as a biological determinant. This tends to connote some sort of Darwinian 'purity' which surely does not exist. Banton[62] argues that individuals may utilise physical and cultural characteristics in order to create groups and categories by the process of inclusion and exclusion.[63] Where this occurs in relation to 'race', it goes against the essence of inclusiveness that the directive desires. The use of the term 'ethnicity' comes some way to meet this concern. Lustgarten[64] says that it is an anthropological term devised as an alternative to 'race' to avoid any connotation of innate biological differences. From a legal point of view ethnicity means the ancestry of individual forebears—a socially and distinct minority group. Such social distinctions are more a function of culture than pigmentation.

In its effort to move away from these difficulties the directive sees fit to prohibit any reference to 'race' or ethnicity except in so far as it serves to further the needs of 'genuine occupational qualifications'[65] or 'positive action' programmes.[66] The directive promotes as the only moral principle that of equal treatment in decisions, which essentially concern the distribution, or redistribution of resources. The positive aspects of such provision is that those charged with allocating resources are under a duty to think about the criteria they use in order to pursue such activity, accept that it is legally wrong to allocate

61. See para 6 Council Directive 2000/43/EC.

62. M. Banton, *Racial and Ethnic Competition* (Cambridge University Press, 1983)

63. Banton, ch.6.

64. *Op. cit.* p. 76-82.

65. Article 4 Council Directive 2000/43/EC.

66. Article 5 Council Directive 2000/43/EC.

resources on any other basis than equality and act to avoid infringing the law.

In Germany, Britain and France this would mean that in the public housing sector, for instance, authorities would have to look at the criteria for housing allocation more closely. There has been a tendency to 'ghettoise' areas by allocating poor run down housing to third country nationals. Many live in substandard housing and are segregated from the 'dominant' population.[67] Such policies add to the isolation and the perception of discrimination and unfair treatment. As one Turkish gang member said of the distance between Germans and Turkish people, '...no government...speaks for us and we cannot identify with the state.... I will never be able to support a government which is hostile to me. Instead, I just find my own people and try to make my own rules and follow laws that suit us.'[68] A Community provision which imposes on member states a duty to allocate housing (and other) resources on the basis of equality would go some way towards alleviating the problem of discrimination—although there is no guarantee that third country nationals would receive better housing, rather that they would be treated equally in terms of allocation.[69]

Where this directive does fall down is on providing a positive duty to provide suitable housing except in so far as such a policy might be allowed for under the positive action provision in Article 5.[70] This provision states that, '*With a view to ensuring full equality in practice, the principle of equal treatment shall not prevent any Member State from maintaining or adopting specific measures to prevent or compensate for disadvantages linked to racial or ethnic origin.*' However this article does not impose a positive duty that is legally enforceable, rather it is a weak attempt to support those member states that wish to keep in place (or develop) positive action programmes. But at least there is the recognition that positive action measures may be necessary to provide quick and perhaps temporary solutions to historically structured patterns of discrimination experienced by third country nationals.

A far more pressing problem is the identification of the beneficiaries of these anti-discrimination measures. Who are the individuals that should be targeted? At first blush, it may seem obvious. The beneficiaries must be those who suffer discrimination in terms of jobs, housing and so on because they have

---

67. Kolinsky *op. cit.* p. 103. A.G. Hargreaves, *op. cit.* p. 32.

68. Kolinsky, *op. cit.* p. xx.

69. The implication here is that where all people receive bad housing on an equal basis there is no recourse to a legal remedy, since there is no legally recognised discrimination.

70. Council Directive 2000/43/EC.

been identified as belonging to separate racial or ethnic groups. But there are a number of individuals that may claim to be part of a discriminated against ethnic or 'racial' group whom one would not have thought of as falling within the remit of the provisions. The slogan 'German for the Germans'[71] has been current in Germany's post reunification. 'Ethnic' Germans may make a claim that they are not being treated equally on the basis of race or ethnicity compared with Slav, Jewish or black Germans when it comes to housing allocation for instance.

The difficulty with this analysis when applied to the various member states is compounded by the fact that not only is the notion of race and ethnicity unclear, there are a number of member states that do not share this 'Americanised' view of race relations that seems to have shaped EU policy. Whilst some member states such as the UK are used to the language of race and ethnicity—indeed a whole race relations industry has been built on such notions- the same cannot be said of countries such as Germany and France.

Amongst the issues that face France in terms of 'race relations' is the difficulty of recognising racial or ethnic groups at all. The general view is that in France you are either French or not. If you are not French in France, this is due to *your* failure to integrate. The trend is very much towards blaming tension between groups differently perceived on the basis of *their* failure to become French. Hargreaves[72] argues that until the recently the trend was to equate integration with assimilation, i.e. '...the wholesale elimination of differences through the generalisation of pre-existing national norms.'[73] It was incidents such as the challenge to the system in 1989 by three North Africans school girls: excluded from their school in northern France because they insisted upon wearing their 'Muslim' headscarves in class,[74] that forced the hand of some French policy makers to reconsider the notion of integration. However, as Hargreaves[75] points out, this falls far short of positively recognising racial or ethnic difference. The dominant policy approach has been one of 'co-option', i.e. to tolerate differences by seeking to ensure minorities limit

71. N. Piper, *Racism, Nationalism and Citizenship. Ethnic Minorities in Britain and Germany* (Aldershot, Ashgate, 1998) p. 167.

72. Hargreaves, *op. cit.* p. 32.

73. *Ibid.* p. 33.

74. S. Poulter, *Ethnicity, Law and Human Rights* (London, Oxford, 1999), pp. 386-7. An added factor was that French schools have a long tradition of secularism.

75. Hargreaves, *op. cit.* p. 205.

their distinctive patterns of behaviour in ways compatible with dominant cultural norms. In the context of France then the Race Directive should at least force the issue of recognising that different treatment on the basis of ethnicity is discriminatory. The limitation here of course is that the claims by Muslims and others for their culture or ethnicity to be recognised and protected is not one that will be resolved by the directive as it currently stands since the essence of this instrument is to ignore ethnic difference in favour of the equal treatment principle.[76]

Very different considerations exist in Germany where, unless one can show genealogical roots stemming several centuries, it would seem, one cannot call oneself German. Turkish and other people may be settled in Germany in term of rights to work and reside, but they will never be German. Generally speaking, says Kolinsky neither long term residents nor their offspring born in Germany acquire a right of citizenship.[77] However, there is a distinct, if not deliberate, failure to link the idea of what it means to be German with racist ideology. It is said that there are the 'true' Germans and the rest, the '*auslandische Arbeitnehmer*'—foreign members of the workforce or '*auslandische Mitburger*—foreigners next door.[78] What this is not linked to are policies of deliberate exclusion based, in the main, on 'racial' preference.[79] The Race Directive may serve to clarify in the minds of the German legislature and judiciary, if not that of the public, that certain views of foreigners and the negative conduct that is likely to flow from such may be racially discriminatory. Like the French example, one of the difficulties is recognising that cultural/ethnic difference can and should be treated equally and that the merit principle, on its own, cannot provide the panacea. The definition of a racial or ethnic group may need better clarity if it is to serve as the means by which a legal system is to consider claims for equality. Moreover, a legal system must have a better

76. Another problems for Muslims in particular is whether they will be recognised as a ethnic or religious group. Council Directive 2000/78/EC prohibits religious discrimination but is limited in its scope to employment and occupation. The Race Directive, which is wider in scope may not apply to Muslims who face racial discrimination if they are not recognised as a 'racial' or ethnic group.

77. The right to German citizenship changed from the 1 January 2000 there will be entitlement provided certain requirements have been met. See http://www.german.../reform_of_the_nationality_law.htm.

78. Kolinsky, *op. cit.* p. xii.

79. See N. Piper, *op. cit.*

means of considering the idea that ethnic or cultural differences should be welcomed rather than shunned.

SUPPORT MECHANISMS

No matter how much law exists in theory, one measure of its effectiveness is whether or not those who are likely to benefit from it can use it. There should be some way of predicting difficulties of access. Such issues are reflected in the Race Directive under the heading 'Remedies and Enforcement'.[80] These mechanisms[81] include provision for the defence of rights[82] and victimisation.[83]

Defence of Rights

Article 7(2) provides that *'Member States shall ensure that associations, organisations or other legal entities, which have, in accordance with the criteria laid down by their national law, a legitimate interest in ensuring that the provisions of this Directive are complied with, may engage, either on behalf or in support of the complainant, with his or her approval, in any judicial and/or administrative procedure provided for the enforcement of obligations under this Directive*

This provision focuses on the right of third party support for complainants. A person who alleges that there has been racial or ethnic discrimination or harassment can obtain support from associations or organisations. The association or organisation can also act on behalf of the complainant. Such a mechanism of support has proved fruitful in the context of British race-relations litigation. In the watershed case of *Mandla v Dowell Lee*[84] it was the relatively well-resourced Commission for Racial Equality[85] that took the case through the British legal system culminating in a decision by the House of Lords that Sikhs are an ethnic group, thus protected by the Race Relations Act 1976. The requirements of Article 7(2) appear to provide potential litigants with a means

80. Chapter II Council Directive 2000/43/EC.
81. By Article 6 Council Directive 2000/43/EC where member states have measures in place more favourable they are prohibited from reducing the level of protection.
82. Article 7 Council Directive 2000/43/EC.
83. Article 9 Council Directive 2000/43/EC.
84. [1982] 3 All ER 1108; [1983] 2 AC 548.
85. A statutory body set up to oversee specific race relations measures endowed with powers of enforcement and the right to make recommendations for change.

by which they could realistically access the legal and/or administrative systems that must be set up to ensure that the obligations under the directive are complied with.[86] Some member states, namely Britain, are very familiar with such organisational support mechanisms.

However, Article 7(2) falls a little short of what one would expect of a provision designed to ensure that complainants obtain appropriate support in this sense. The organisations that appear to have a right to bring action on behalf of litigants or support them in bringing complaints must be recognised as *legal entities*. The provision specifically states that, *'Member States shall ensure that associations, organisations or other legal entities...'*[87] may act on behalf of complainants. The problem with the words '...legal entity...' implies that third parties must have legal personality. Whilst it is perfectly reasonable to expect associations and organisations to bear legal personality when involved in legal litigation it is unclear why there should be a legal personality requirement when engaging, '*...either on behalf or in support of the complainant...*' more generally. Another difficulty is the meaning to be attached to the requirement that the association or organisation must have a *'legitimate interest'*. There is no indication of what that means bar that of ensuring that the provisions of the directive are complied with.[88] One can see why the Council of Ministers and Commission would seek to dissuade those who might use this provision to bring vexatious and frivolous complaints,[89] but the use of such vague notions in an area where precision is likely to be decisive may undermine the effectiveness of the provision. Given that the directive is aimed at providing a common framework, which imposes a duty on member states to bring in effective anti-discrimination legislation, it is unfortunate that there is such ambiguity. One hopes that member states will take to the *spirit* rather than the *letter* of this provision but in reality, arguments are generally two-sided. Much may be made of the ambiguity of this requirement, which may serve to undermine its importance for complainants.

Perhaps the most problematic issue with Article 7(2) is that it does not impose on member states the positive duty to ensure that there are organisa-

86. By Article 7(1) Council Directive 2000/43/EC, member states must ensure that there are judicial and administrative systems in place for all persons who consider themselves wronged by failure to apply the principle of equal treatment.

87. Article 7(2) Council Directive 2000/43/EC.

88. *Ibid.* Article 7(2)

89. Although some might argue that this is a bit of a red herring.

tions that not only support litigants but can also act independently. The provision only bites where organisations have the consent of the person aggrieved. A more comprehensive provision would need to give such organisations the right to bring cases under their own prerogative. The failure to require member states to create the organisational infrastructure to support litigants as well as bring cases in their own right is likely to lead to disparity between the various member states. A more meaningful provision would be one that imposed a positive duty to ensure that such organisational infrastructure with the requisite powers was brought into existence.

Victimisation

As part of the recognition of the stigmatisation and 'blame culture' that appears to prevail in various member states towards people who suffer from racial or ethnic discrimination and harassment, the Race Directive has given legal effect to the notion of victimisation. Article 9 provides that

> Member States shall introduce into their national legal systems such measures as are necessary to protect individuals from any adverse treatment or adverse consequence as a reaction to a complainant or to proceedings aimed at enforcing compliance with the principle of equal treatment.[90]

Unlike Article 7, Article 9 appears to impose a positive duty on member states to provide a legal remedy for those who may be victimised for bringing complaints. The reach of this provision seems to be wide since it relates to protection of, '*. . . individuals from any adverse treatment or adverse consequence . . .*' the key word *any* has the potential to catch a wide variety of conduct from whatever source. The provision also expressly supports complainants where there is an intention to victimise (adverse treatment) and where there is no intention, or it cannot be proved, (adverse consequence). There is no requirement that the source of the complaint be the person against whom an initial complaint has been brought. Thus in the context of a complaint about a housing, service provision or employment practice where it may be difficult to prove that the person or institution against whom the complaint has been made is also victimising the complainant, a case could be brought providing there is evidence of adverse treatment.

Herein lies a problem—the problem of causation. How is the complainant to link the adverse treatment to the fact that a complaint has been made con-

90. Council Directive 2000/43/EC.

tending that there has been unequal treatment? Presumably, regardless of the source of the adverse treatment, there must be a causal relationship between the original complaint and the fact that the complainant has suffered as a consequence of raising the issue, otherwise the provision would be so wide as to be unworkable. This issue of causation arose in the British case of *Aziz* v *Trinity Street Taxis*.[91] Aziz, an Asian taxicab proprietor and member of an association of taxicab operators, complained that he was being unfairly treated in the amount he was asked to pay to have a third taxi admitted to the associations' radio system. He secretly recorded conversations with other taxi drivers and was unsuccessful in bringing a case in the industrial tribunal. As a result of that case, the secret recordings were revealed. Subsequently Aziz was expelled from the association. He brought a complaint that his expulsion led to victimisation since it was because of the secret recordings that he was expelled. The court held that the expulsion did not amount to victimisation since this '... contemplates a motive which is consciously connected with the race relations legislation—here that fact did not influence them in expelling him'[92] since the same action would have been taken against any person who had disclosed confidential information.

Such reasoning, argues Townshend-Smith, makes the provisions on victimisation vulnerable to severe criticism.[93] Victimisers have an effective defence if they can prove[94] that they would have treated any person in the same way regardless of race or ethnicity. In other words, victimisers could rely on the principle of treating all people equally in order to undermine the principle of equal treatment in relation to race or ethnicity.

Despite its limitations the fact that victimisation has been recognised as a potential problem for complainants, and that member states are under a duty to ensure that complainants obtain adequate protection, should go some way towards the desire that a provision such as the Race Directive should be effective.

---

91. [1988] IRLR 204, CA.

92. *Aziz* v *Trinity Street Taxis* [1988] IRLR 204, CA, per Slade LJ, pp. 210-211.

93. R.J. Townshend-Smith, *Discrimination Law: Text, Cases and Materials* (London, Cavendish, 1998).

94. The burden of proof has been partially shifted to the respondent. According to Article 8 Council Directive 2000/43/EC, the complainant only has to provide facts from which it may be presumed that there has been discrimination.

Conclusion

The Race Directive attempts to provide Community law rights for people who suffer racism, racial or ethnic discrimination, harassment or victimisation to bring a complaint. Individuals have been given the right to challenge provisions at member state level that are contrary to the equal treatment of racial or ethnic groups. The corollary of legal rights is the creation of legal obligations. Member states are obligated under this common framework directive to provide the legal and administrative structure that will give effect to the equal treatment principle as regards anti-race discrimination. They must provide sanctions for infringement of the national provisions adopted to take account of the Race Directive that are, '...*effective, proportionate and dissuasive*.'[95] Following on from this there is provision in the directive for the Community institutions: European Parliament and the Council, to consider the application of the directive. This provision is vital if the Community is to build up a reservoir of information regarding the working of the directive and the need for revision.[96]

There is much to commend the directive as a model providing legal rights and obligations across divergent cultural and political systems. The Race Directive is a flexible tool that can be fashioned to legal systems with different historical traditions—common and civil law, yet it speaks for those people within these legal systems who are victims of racism and racial or ethnic discrimination. The Race Directive is a 'one size fits all' but not a 'once and for all' legal instrument. It has only begun to take its first steps. There are provisions within this instrument that allow it to be fashioned in ways that are more appropriate as its influence grows. Such an instrument may well provide a useful starting point for universal legal measures.

95. Article 15 Council Directive 2000/43/EC.

96. Article 17(1) and (2) Council Directive 2000/43/EC makes provision for revision and update of the directive on a regular basis.

Bibliography

European Monitoring Centre, *Looking Reality in the Face, Annual Report 1998* (Vienna, EUMC, 1998).

European Monitoring Centre, *Giving Europe a Soul,* (Vienna, EUMC, 1998).

A.G. Hargreaves, *Immigration, 'Race' and Ethnicity in Contemporary France,* (London, Routledge, 1995).

C. Wihtol de Wenden, 'North African Immigration and the French Political Imaginary', in M. Silverman (ed) *Race, Discourse and Power in France,* (Aldershot, Avebury, 1991).

L. Lustgarten, *Legal Control of Racial Discrimination* (London, MacMillan, 1980).

Palmer, Moon and Cox, *Discrimination at Work,* (London, LAG, 1997).

B. Bercusson, *European Labour Law,* (London, Butterworths, 1996).

D. Horrocks and E. Kolinsky (eds), *Turkish Culture in German Society Today,* (Oxford, Berghahn Books, 1996).

J. Gabriel, *Racism, Culture, Markets,* (London, Routledge,

J. Solomos, *Race and Racism in Britain,* (London, MacMillan, 1993).

R.J. Townshend-Smith, *Discrimination Law: Text, Cases and Materials,* (London. Cavendish, 1998).

P. Gilroy, *Small Acts,* (London, Serpents' Tail, 1994).

G. Ford, *Report Drawn up on behalf of the Committee of Inquiry into Racism and Xenophobia,* (Luxembourg, Office of Official Publications of E.C. 1991).

I. Harvey and G. Simmons, *The French National Front* (USA, Westview Pass, 1996).

European Commission Against Racism and Intolerance Newsletter no. 1. July 1999.

W.D. Chapin, *Germany for the Germans? The Political Effects of International Migration,* (London, Greenwood Press, 1997).

H. Booth, *The Migration Process in Britain and West Germany,* (Aldershot, Avebury, 1992).

M. Spencer, *States of Injustice,* (London, Pluto Press, 1995).

B. Parekh, *Rethinking Multiculturalism. Cultural Diversity and Political Theory,* Hampshire, Macmillan Press, 2000).

A. Dummett, *Citizens and Foreigners,* (London, CRE, 1994).

S. Poulter, *Ethnicity, Law and Human Rights. The English Experience,* (Oxford, Oxford University Press, 1999).

J. Dine and B. Watt (eds), *Discrimination Law. Concepts, Limitations and Justifications,* (London, Longman, 1996).

P. Craig and G. De Burca, *EU Law. Text, Cases and Materials,* (Oxford, Oxford University Press, 1998).

The Drafting of the Articles on the Middle East and Antisemitism at the Durban Conference against Racism

Raphael Walden*

The World Conference Against Racism, or, to give it its full name, the World Conference against Racism, Racial Discrimination, Xenophobia and Related Intolerance, was held in Durban on 31 August—7 September 2001, having been convened by the General Assembly of the United Nations. It was the third such conference, the first two having been held in 1978 and 1983. Both of these earlier ones failed, largely because of the previous adoption by the General Asembly of Resolution 3379, (the 'Zionism is Racism' Resolution) which made consensus impossible.

As is the case with all UN Conferences, this one required a great deal of preparation, starting a year and a half in advance. The aim of any major world conference, e.g. the Vienna Conference on Human Rights or the Beijing Conference on Women, is to bring about the adoption of a text which reflects

---

* Solicitor. Former Israeli Ambassador. Adviser to the CCJO on UN and International Affairs.

Raphael Walden (ed.), Racism and Human Rights, *165-176.*

the widest possible consensus, given all the conflicting claims and interests involved, and this requires extensive preliminary negotiation. All this could not be done just in the one week during which the Conference itself was held. So much of the work had to be done beforehand.

A key aspect of the Conference was the role played by NGOs. Although the primary participants in UN Conferences are the 191 States that are members of the United Nations, NGOs have been playing an ever-greater role in their proceedings. Quite apart from any influence they may have behind the scenes, they are often accorded rights, to a greater or lesser degree, to circulate papers at meetings and even to address them. In addition, in order to satisfy their wish for their voice to be more fully heard, major intergovenmental conferences are very often accompanied by a parallel NGO Forum. Both the main Intergovernmental Conference and the NGO Forum regularly adopt lengthy documents, each covering the same themes from different perspectives, one intended to reflect the concerns of governments, the other those of international civil society. This also happened at Durban, where the week long government conference was preceded by an NGO Forum, which lasted the same length of time. Thus the Durban Conference was actually two distinct though inter-related events.

The impetus for the Conference came from African countries, which were eager for it to address the inter-related topics of colonialism, historical slavery, and anti-black discrimination. They were joined by many other victim groups, such as migrants, Dalits, gypsies, and a whole range of others, all anxious for their concerns to be addressed. These issues ought to have been the major topics of Conference debates; in the event, though, the disproportionate amount of time taken up there as well as at the NGO Forum by the anti—Israeli lobby, meant that African and other issues had the amount of time devoted to them, especially at the intergovernmental Conference, significantly curtailed.

The preliminary work for the Conference took the form of a number of meetings in Geneva, in the form of both informal working groups and official preparatory committees, in which both states and NGOs took part. Their purpose was to generate by degrees a document in which as much as possible could be discussed and agreed in advance, so that what was left for Durban were those issues, hopefully as few as possible, which required negotiation and compromise at a higher level. The two official preparatory committees were held in Geneva on 1-5 May 2000 and 21 May—1 June 2000.

What was particularly influential for the outcome was the decision to follow the common practice of preceding the global conference by regional ones, so that each of the main areas of the world would be able to input its own perspectives into the document as a whole. Regional conferences were held in Europe, Africa, Latin America and Asia.

The difficulties began with the Asian Conference. Pressure from Arab and Islamic States led to its being held in Teheran, hardly a neutral venue, as was demonstrated by the initial refusal to allow any Jewish NGO to attend (and this, it should be noted, at a Conference dedicated to combating racism). This continued until the very last moment, when the Iranian Government made a show of relenting, but too late for visas to be obtained in time.

The document produced at the Asian meeting contained many of the characteristic themes of the conference with regard to Israel. Many of the paragraphs on Israel resembled those produced routinely at UN meetings, such as the General Assembly and the Human Rights Commission. The difference, though, was that this meeting was on the specific topic of racism. The very act, therefore, of including criticisms of Israel implied that it was being condemned as a racist country. This amounted, by implication, to the revival of the 'Zionism = Racism' allegation 10 years after it had been revoked by the General Assembly, and despite the categorical assertion by Secretary General Kofi Annan that it was defunct.

The Teheran document contained the following assertions:

- Foreign occupation is a form of racism
- The foreign occupation of Jerusalem with all its racial practices should be brought to an end
- Foreign occupation, its laws based on racial discrimination, constitute a new form of apartheid, a crime against humanity, a form of genocide, and a serious threat to international peace and security.
- There should be a cessation of all the practices of racial discrimination to which the Palestinians and other inhabitants of the other territories occupied by Israel are subjected.
- The problem of Palestinian refugees is linked to the 'racial practices of the occupying power' and the Law of Return (which gives all Jews the right of Israeli citizenship) is said to be racially biased.

Here we have, in an early form, some of the main themes which were to reappear in subsequent drafts. Israel is linked to racism, to genocide, and to apartheid (a particularly effective allegation at a conference held in South Africa).

These texts, which passed through various drafts all the way to Durban, were one prong of a two-pronged attack. The other was the systematic attempt to downplay and dilute, and indeed even eliminate, references that had been contained in early drafts to the Holocaust and to anti-Semitism. These references derived from texts which had emanated from other Regional Conferences, notably the European one held in Strasbourg. So far as the Holocaust was concerned, constant amendments were proposed by the Arab Group, whose spokesmen were chiefly the Syrian, Pakistani and Palestinian representatives, to replace 'Holocaust' in the singular and with a capital H by 'holocausts' in the plural and with a small H, thereby implying that it was just one of many holocausts, and by implication nothing special. In fact, this was not merely implied, but stated in so many words by the representatives of those and like-minded countries. This demand was firmly opposed by all the members of the Western Group. At the end of one of the sessions in Geneva, the Swedish Ambassador, speaking on behalf of the European Union, made a statement in which he said: 'Some of the comments presented during this week on the subject of the Holocaust are unacceptable to us. We want to remind delegations that the Holocaust was a tragedy with unique characteristics, and has been given this specific name of 'The Holocaust' which should be applied exclusively to this European tragedy.'

There were also many attempts to minimise or exclude references to anti-Semitism. This was done in various ways, one of which was to refuse to allow any mention of it at all, unless accompanied by references to Islamophobia or Arabophobia. The other, much more radical line was to try and appropriate the very concept. Thus, some of the drafts put forward by Arab States contained such expressions as 'Zionist practices against Semitism' and 'Zionist anti-Semitism'. The argument, which was heard time after time, was that Arabs were Semites, and so anything that could be construed as hostile to Arabs was therefore anti-Semitic.

In both cases, what could be observed was the attempt to take over the specific terms used to describe injustices committed against Jews, while playing down or even denying the existence of those very injustices. Zionism, or Israeli policies, were to be regarded as racism; anti-Semitism was not, and indeed the concept in its usual sense was dismissed as meaningless.

Thus, by the end of the preparatory processes in Geneva, and indeed long before that, it became clear that the determination of some States to force the Middle East issue onto the agenda, while removing the Holocaust and anti-Semitism from it, together with the introduction of extreme and one sided language, were likely to be stumbling blocks in the path to a satisfactory outcome.

All this relates to the drafting history of the Government document. As regards the NGO document, the initial text was prepared by Sangoco, the South African NGO umbrella organisation. This body played an extremely unhelpful role throughout the proceedings of the Conference; it did all it could to further the agenda just described, including the commission of a great many procedural irregularities. To illustrate its attitude, before the conference started, the representatives of Sangoco went to the Middle East, to be briefed on the situation. They were received by the Palestinian Authority in Gaza, but when it was suggested that they should also meet Israeli representatives, they refused to do so. Again, when the NGO Forum started in Durban, the Head of Sangoco, who presided, wore a Palestinian scarf, and promised that the Forum would be a vehicle for Palestinian claims.

However, all this was a mere preliminary to what happened in Durban itself.

To understand the events at Durban, some stage-setting is necessary. The meetings hitherto had all taken place in the restrained environment of the United Nations building in Geneva. Although NGO representatives were present, they could operate only within parameters of the privileges which they were accorded there. It was different in Durban. There, as has already been indicated, NGOs held a parallel Forum separate from the Government Conference. A huge number, many thousands in fact, participated. This was made possible by the extremely liberal right of participation granted. At most UN meetings only those NGOs that have consultative status with ECOSOC, the Economic and Social Council, have the right to take part. But at this Conference virtually every NGO that applied, both national and international, was given the right of participation. Only a handful of NGOs had their application refused, owing to the specific opposition of individual states. In order to make this number manageable, the NGOs grouped themselves into 'caucuses' i.e. groupings with common interests. One of those was the Jewish caucus, made up of the many Jewish organisations that had come.

In order to accommodate this enormous number of participants, the Kingsmead cricket stadium was taken over, and marquees were set up in which meetings could be held, and written and other materials displayed, among them, many of the articles published in this volume. Most of the NGOs participating similarly circulated material furthering their causes in serious and positive terms. But not, alas, all. An organisation called the Arab Lawyers Union distributed a booklet containing caricatures of Jews with fangs and hooked noses, blood dripping from their mouths, which looked as though they had been taken straight out of 1930s Nazi propaganda leaflets. Another organisation circulated a picture of Hitler with the caption 'What would have happened if I [i.e. Hitler] had won? NO Israel and NO Palestinian bloodshed'.

At the Youth Summit, which took place at the beginning of the Forum, there were shouts of 'you don't belong to the human race, you are a cursed people, the Jews killed Christ' and so on.

About the second day of the Conference, the World Union of Jewish Students, having seen the amount of anti-Zionist and openly anti-Semitic material there was around, set up a table at which Jewish material, T-shirts, booklets etc, was distributed. This provoked a constant noisy and vociferous confrontation with groups of Arabs and Arab-supporters, who did not try to engage in dialogue, keeping up instead chants of 'Zionism is Racism'. When one of the Jewish students, who was wearing a kippah (skullcap), tried to talk to one of the Arabs, the latter said 'I won't talk to you until you take that off', pointing to his kippah. Compare the response that would have been evoked if a Jew had said to an Arab 'I won't talk to you unless you take off your kaffiyeh'.

Finally, one further episode must be mentioned. On the penultimate day of the Conference, a massive pro-Palestinian and anti-Israeli march was held in Durban. This was accompanied by the distribution of the same kind of anti-Semitic literature that we have already referred to, but on this occasion it also included the well-known anti-Semitic forgery 'the Protocols of the elders of Zion', this without any interference from the authorities. The march went past and remained at the Durban Jewish Club, where the Jewish caucus met, and forced the club, for security reasons, to remain closed for several hours.

While all this was going on in the background, the work of drafting the NGO Forum's document was proceeding. The method adopted was that each caucus of NGOs should hold a meeting in order to prepare a text on the issue or issues that concerned it, and that the text as a whole should then be considered by a general drafting committee. It was agreed, not without difficulty, that the Jewish caucus should prepare a text on anti-Semitism.

The meeting on anti-Semitism accordingly started. Three statements were made without incident. However, shortly after the fourth speaker, the President of the International Union of Jewish Students, started his address, a group of Palestinians and pro-Palestinians began shouting down the speaker and the chairman with a degree of verbal violence which verged on the physical. This forced the meeting to break up. It took about half an hour to get the chaotic scene under control, so that the meeting could be resumed. Ultimately this became possible and the second half commenced. Finally, a text emerged representing the outcome of the discussions which was handed to the drafting committee. This was not the end of the matter, however. During a night meeting of the Jewish NGOs a message was received from the Steering Committee of the NGO Forum to say that that the text was being challenged by certain Jewish representatives who claimed that the Jewish caucus did not represent them. The challenge in fact came from a well known Israeli anti-Zionist, who as far as anyone knows represented no one but himself. The steering committee in the end rejected the complaint.

The next day, there was a repetition of the same scenario. Jewish NGOs tried to hold a press conference. The speakers made their statements, but when the time came for journalists to ask questions, the same barracking started, together with the chanting of the mantra 'Zionism is Racism', by a group of non-journalists who had forced their way in. The result was that the journalists present were unable to ask any questions, and the press conference was broken up.

All this was a prelude to the final act, the adoption of the Declaration and Programme of Action by the NGO Forum. Its adoption was marked by many procedural irregularities, so much so that even after the event it was unclear what had been adopted, and the final text was not made available until considerably after the end of the conference. The text included without question the sections drafted by each of the 'caucuses' of NGOs on their respective concerns. The only exception was the section on anti-Semitism drafted by the Jewish caucus. When this came up for the vote, a representative, speaking, regrettably, on behalf of the World Council of Churches, proposed the deletion of a key clause in the anti-Semitism text. This was the clause which stated that equating Zionism with Racism, de-legitimising Jewish self determination, and targeting Jews for violence because of their support for Israel, were forms of anti-Semitism. The World Council of Churches proposal was adopted, and at that point the Jewish caucus walked out en bloc. This was a very visible act, and its departure was accompanied by shouts of 'get out', 'go' and so on.

Some indication must be given of what the NGO document contained on the topics of Israel and Zionism. The passages cannot be quoted in full, because they go on for several pages, but the following is an outline.

- Art. 98: Israel is accused of 'racist methods amounting to Israel's brand of apartheid and other racist crimes against humanity'.
- Art. 99: Israel is accused of 'acts of genocide and practices of ethnic cleansing, a racist system which is Israel's brand of apartheid'.

- Art. 160 This refers to 'Israeli systematic perpetration of racist crimes including war crimes, acts of genocide and ethnic cleansing...'.
- Art. 162. This asserts 'We declare Israel as a racist, apartheid state'.
- As for the plan of action, only quotation at length can supply its full flavour, and again only quotes and summaries can be given:
- Art. 417: Calls for ... all measures employed against the South African Apartheid Regime [to be employed against Israel].
- Art. 418: Calls for the reinstitution of UN Resolution 3379 determining the practices of Zionism as racist practices
- Art. 419 Calls for the establishment of a war crimes tribunal to investigate and bring to justice those who may be guilty of war crimes, acts of genocide and ethnic cleansing and the crime of Apartheid which amount to crimes against humanity that have been or continue to be perpetrated in Israel and the Occupied Arab Territories.
- Art. 424 Calls upon the international community to impose a policy of complete and total isolation of Israel as an apartheid state as in the case of South Africa which means the imposition of mandatory and comprehensive sanctions and embargoes, the full cessation of all links ... between all States and Israel. Call upon the Government of South Africa to take the lead in this policy of isolation ....
- Art. 425 Provides for the condemnation of those states who are supporting, aiding and abetting the Israeli Apartheid state and its perpetration of racist crimes against humanity including ethnic cleansing, acts of genocide.

Another set of articles relates to 'Zionist anti-Semitism'.

- Preamble 46: 'Concerned that anti-Arab racism is another form of anti-Semitism and Islamophobia that have led to violence and hate crimes'.
- Preamble 79 'Arabs as a Semitic people have also suffered from alternative forms of anti-Semitism manifesting itself as anti-Arab discrimination ....'

A large number of NGOs, particularly from the East European Group, issued a letter dissociating themselves from the NGO document. In fact, the language was so extreme that Mary Robinson, the UN High Commissioner for Human Rights, for the first time ever, so far as we are aware, at a UN Conference, refused to recommend it for adoption to the subsequent Government Conference.

The Government Conference

When the NGO Forum came to an end, the Government Conference started. This was naturally a far more orderly event. Unlike the NGO Forum, which, as stated, was held in tents in a cricket stadium, the Government Conference was held in the Durban Conference centre, a building set up expressly for such events. Security was extremely tight, and it was quite impossible to get in without a pass. Furthermore, only one representative of each NGO, whether large or small, was allowed to enter at a time, so that the number of those other than state representatives who could get in was restricted. This meant that there was far less opportunity for incidents of the kind that took place at the NGO Conference. However, so far as the content of the Government Conference's Programme and Plan of Action were concerned, exactly the same issues arose, but in a more significant form, inasmuch as an instrument adopted by Governments carries far more weight than one adopted by NGOs.

The draft presented at the beginning of the Conference contained proposals by Arab States in much the same language as that of the NGO text, not surprisingly, since it emanated from the same source. Initially, at the preliminary stages of the conference, a draft had been prepared by the Secretariat, i.e. by the High Commissioner's office. This was strongly repudiated, above all by the African Group, on the grounds that it closely reflected the Strasbourg text emanating from the European Group, and did not sufficiently acknowledge African concerns. The Secretariat's input having been repudiated early on, subsequent drafts for discussion took the form of compilations of suggestions made by different regional groups and individual States. It was only later, much nearer the conference itself, that actual negotiation started on the texts, but by the time it began, there were still a very large number of articles that had not yet been resolved, quite apart from what were referred to as the main controversial issues, i.e. the question of compensation for victims of colonialism, and above all the Middle East issues.

The Western countries, namely the E.U., the U.S.A. Canada, Australia and New Zealand as well as some other supporters, made it absolutely clear that they would not compromise on the extreme language demanded by the Arab/Islamic bloc. The USA, in particular, had been in two minds all along about whether to participate in the Conference at all. Initially it decided to come, though not at the highest level (i.e. not at the level of the Secretary of State, Colin Powell). However, as the conference proceeded and there seemed to be no willingness to compromise on the part of the Arab states, the US decided to pull out. Israel for its part had been in two minds about participation all along. Some in the Government were in favour of participation, on the grounds that the arena ought not to be abandoned, others against , arguing that this would appear to be giving the conference a seal of approval. In the end Israel did participate, though not at a ministerial level, but after a few days walked out, together with most Jewish organisations. There was also talk of other Western countries pulling out, but in the end they did not do so.

During the course of the Conference, the issues of anti-Semitism, the Holocaust and the Middle East were put into the hands of a small negotiating group, which met behind the scenes, but this did not stop the Arab representatives from constantly raising them at the open committee meetings. This meant that at the Conference itself, as throughout the preliminary meetings, an inordinate amount of time was spent on these issues, although they had nothing to do with a conference on racism at all, and the time devoted to the many real themes of the conference was significantly curtailed.

About two days before the conference came to an end, a compromise package text (which in fact had been drafted by the secretariat) was submitted to the delegates by the South African Presidency on these issues. It eliminated the extreme language which was contained in the original drafts of the Government document and in the final texts of the NGO Forum, and to this extent was positive. Its provisions in summary were:

- It was said that The Holocaust must never be forgotten
- Concern was expressed for the existence of religious intolerance
- Concern was expressed for the increase of anti-Semitism and Islamophobia
- Concern was expressed about the plight of the Palestinian people under foreign occupation.
- Recognition was expressed of 'the inalienable right of the Palestinian people to self-determination and to the establishment of an independent state' and of 'the right to security for all States in the region including Israel'. All states were called upon to support the peace process.
- There was a call for a just, comprehensive and lasting peace in the region.
- Recognition of 'the right of refugees to return voluntarily to their homes and properties'.

This was the text that was ultimately adopted.

What can be said about it?

On the positive side, the extreme formulations originally proposed were eliminated. There is no reference to 'Zionist anti-Semitism', 'genocide', 'Zionist apartheid', and 'Zionist racism'. The demand for a Palestinian State which was included belongs to the language of policy and not to that of scurrility and abuse. The Holocaust as a unique event is allowed to have existed. The evil of anti-Semitism is acknowledged. On the other hand these single references to the Holocaust and to anti-Semitism are the only ones in the entire document, and are included in a section on the Middle East, where they have no place at all. And above all, the very reference to the Middle East dispute in a document about racism, perpetuates the claim that the Arab-Israel dispute is a racial issue, as does the reference to 'The plight of the Palestinian people under foreign occupation' in a section headed 'Victims of Racism, Racial Discrimination, Xenophobia & related Intolerance'.

On the last day a massive attempt was made to reinstate some of the extreme language originally proposed. This failed after hours of intense procedural debate, but as a result of the time taken up by the prolonged discussions, many articles on issues which were of the utmost importance to various groups failed to get adopted, since there was no time left to deal with them. What is more, the original draft contained many more references to the Holocaust and to anti-Semitism in the contexts of the need for education and counteraction, and those fell from the document because of the general decision that texts which were still bracketed by the end of the time limit for discussion would be eliminated. This had the effect of 'killing' not only those references, but also, as has been said, many texts on topics of importance to other interest groups. Thus one effect of the monopolization of much of the discussion by the Arab States was that there were only bare mentions of the Holocaust and of anti-Semitism, and that the Conference was prevented to a large extent from dealing with the issues for which it had in reality been convened.

After the text had been adopted, a number of States made statements. Canada said that the language on the Middle East was ultra vires, a violation of the peace accords, and a significant step backward. The EU in a text submitted later said that the text was only a political document and not legally binding. The Syrian representative speaking from the Arab side said that the holocaust was a great tragedy but was a European event and had nothing to do with the Middle East. He also referred to anti-Semitism as a 'curious concept' (not, apparently a 'curious' reality).

It is time to sum up. The Government document, so far as it goes, contains a great deal of material not related to the Middle East which may serve as a blueprint for subsequent government projects. So far as the Middle East texts in both documents are concerned, they have remained a dead letter, and have never since been referred to. One can only regret that the inordinate amount of time spent on negotiating texts that had nothing to do with the Conference prevented many more relevant issues from being adequately dealt with.

MIX
Papier aus verantwortungsvollen Quellen
Paper from responsible sources
FSC® C105338

If you have any concerns about our products,
you can contact us on
ProductSafety@springernature.com

In case Publisher is established outside the EU,
the EU authorized representative is:
Springer Nature Customer Service Center GmbH
Europaplatz 3, 69115 Heidelberg, Germany

Printed by Libri Plureos GmbH
in Hamburg, Germany

Racism and Human Rights